GIORGIO LEVI DELLA VIDA CONFERENCES

---

Published for the
Gustave E. von Grunebaum Center for Near Eastern Studies
University of California
Los Angeles



NINTH CONFERENCE

# Ethics in Islam

May 6-8, 1983

COMMITTEE

Reverend G. C. Anawati, O.P., Dominican Institute, Cairo

Amin Banani, University of California, Los Angeles

Franz Rosenthal, Yale University

Bertold Spuler, University of Hamburg

Andreas Tietze, University of Vienna

Speros Vryonis, Jr., University of California, Los Angeles

W. Montgomery Watt, University of Edinburgh
*Recipient of the Eighth Giorgio Levi Della Vida Award in Islamic Studies*

NINTH GIORGIO LEVI DELLA VIDA BIENNIAL CONFERENCE
May 6-8, 1983

Gustave E. von Grunebaum Center for Near Eastern Studies
University of California, Los Angeles

# ETHICS IN ISLAM

Edited by
RICHARD G. HOVANNISIAN

The Giorgio Levi Della Vida Medal of the Gustave E. von Grunebaum Center for Near Eastern Studies, University of California, Los Angeles, is awarded biennially to give recognition to an outstanding scholar whose work has significantly and lastingly advanced the study of Islamic civilization. The scholar is selected by a committee appointed by the chancellor of the University of California, Los Angeles, meeting under the chairmanship of the director of the Gustave E. von Grunebaum Center for Near Eastern Studies.

The award carries with it a bronze medal and a prize of money together with the obligation to present in person a formal lecture at the University of California, Los Angeles, as part of a conference. The recipient of the award chooses the theme and selects the other participants to the conference. The proceedings of each conference are published in a special series, of which this volume is the ninth.

The first award was made on May 12, 1967, to Professor Robert Brunschvig of the Sorbonne, Paris, by a committee under the chairmanship of Professor G. E. von Grunebaum, who originated the conference. Subsequent recipients were Professors Joseph Schacht of Columbia, Francesco Gabrieli of the University of Rome, posthumously G. E. von Grunebaum of the University of California, Shlomo Dov Goitein of the Institute for Advanced Study, Princeton, Franz Rosenthal of Yale University, Albert Hourani, University of Oxford, and W. Montgomery Watt, University of Edinburgh.

Eight volumes have been published to date: *Logic in Classical Islamic Culture* (1970), *Theology and Law in Islam* (1971), *Arabic Poetry: Theory and Development* (1973), *Islam and Cultural Change in the Middle Ages* (1975), *Individualism and Conformity in Classical Islam* (1977), *Society and the Sexes in Medieval Islam* (1979), *Islamic Studies: A Tradition and Its Problems* (1980), and *Islam's Understanding of Itself* (1983).

The production editor for this volume was Marina Leasim Preussner, Principal Editor, Gustave E. von Grunebaum Center for Near Eastern Studies.

# ETHICS IN ISLAM

Giorgio Levi Della Vida
1886-1967

# ETHICS IN ISLAM

Edited by

RICHARD G. HOVANNISIAN

1985

UNDENA PUBLICATIONS, MALIBU, CALIFORNIA

Library of Congress Card Number: 85-050721
ISBN: 0-89003-182-7



Undena Publications, P. O. Box 97, Malibu, CA 90265

CONTENTS

# PRESENTATION OF AWARD TO NINTH RECIPIENT, FAZLUR RAHMAN

RICHARD G. HOVANNISIAN
University of California, Los Angeles

Historically, most Muslim jurists made no clear distinction between ethics and law, eventually creating imbalance and tension between the two. The moral and ethical guidelines for human relations in the Qur⁾ān tended to become obscured by the emphasis placed on form and detail in the development of Islamic law. Jurists came to regard the Qur⁾ān as a legal document, and the observance of specific rules and regulations as the fulfillment of divine will. The ethical aspects of the Qur⁾ān were overshadowed by or merged with the legal formulas. It has been suggested that the Qur⁾ān became the prisoner of its interpreters rather than their source and guide.

Among Muslim scholars calling for a return to the ethical spirit of the Qur⁾ān, Fazlur Rahman stands at the forefront. He believes that serious problems were caused by the development of Islamic law outside and away from a solid ethical base. Had law evolved out of ethics, differences of opinion would be grounded more soundly, and there would never have been the need or even the possibility of closing the gates of *ijtihād*. In one of his treatises, Rahman has observed: "Our lawyers often went too far in simply converting rhetorical or ethical statements of the Qur⁾ān into legal ones, while not going far enough in deriving legal norms from verses with an obvious legal import." Only if ethics is distinguished from law, systematized, and made into a self-conscious discipline can law itself properly become a self-conscious discipline.

Professor Rahman's combination of the highest standards of scholarship and his deep personal commitment to the faith and future of Islam has given him a unique position among contemporary scholars and has led to his selection as the ninth recipient of the Giorgio Levi Della Vida award. The vibrations he has created in Islamic studies through his penetrating analyses and advocacy positions have had a ripple effect, making him a point of reference—respected, honored, emulated, and by some rejected and even feared. As a critic of the captivity of Islamic law to form and detail, Rahman speaks from the position of a legal specialist. Over the years he has studied and written about the history, philosophy, practice, and social and economic applications of the law. His profound interest in the problem was reflected in his participation in the second Levi Della Vida conference on "Theology and Law in Islam" and in his choice of the theme "Ethics in Islam" for the ninth biennial conference.

Professor Rahman has had a distinguished career and remains a prolific writer. Receiving his doctorate degree from Oxford University in 1949, he taught at Durham University and at McGill University from 1950 to 1961, served as Director of the Central Institute of Islamic Research in Pakistan from 1962 to 1968, and has been a member of the Department of Near Eastern Languages and Civilizations at the University of Chicago since 1969. He has written ten major books and more than forty articles on Islam and Islamic studies. His most recent contributions include *Major Themes of the Qurʾān* (1980) and *Islam and Modernity: Transformation of an Intellectual Tradition* (1982). Rahman believes that Muslims must come to terms with the challenges of modernism. While secularism is not the answer, Rahman maintains that it is essential to use the knowledge that has been made available through philosophy and the social sciences. A recurring theme in his works is the need to reinterpret Islam in light of ethical and moral thoughts true to the beliefs expressed in the Qurʾān. By systematizing the ethical teachings of the Qurʾān, it will also be possible to construct a conceptual framework for law.

The contributions of Professors Charles Butterworth, Frederick Denny, Kemal Faruki, George Hourani, Wilferd Madelung, and George Makdisi have added richness in breadth and diversity to the theme of "Ethics in Islam." They do honor to the recipient of the ninth Giorgio Levi Della Vida award, Fazlur Rahman.

# LAW AND ETHICS IN ISLAM

FAZLUR RAHMAN
University of Chicago

The Qurʾān regards the conduct of man, individually and collectively, in private and in public, as being under divine command: "Those who do not judge (or decide) in accordance with what God has sent down, these are the disbelievers" (5.44; see also 5.45, 5.47, etc.). Indeed, in 2.213 God's primary purpose in sending revealed books is to decide matters under dispute among people. The Qurʾān, therefore, attributes the commands to prayer or to fast to God, and it is exactly the same with rules concerning financial transactions. Hence Islamic law, from the beginning, was conceived as an indivisible totality in the sense that it was derived from God's Word and thus possessed the same and uniform divine sanction. Some scholars of Islam, both Muslim and non-Muslim, maintain that this characteristic of Islamic law derives from the historical reality. Since there was no government or political ruler in Arabia, as there was, for example, at the birth of Christianity, Muḥammad had to assume the roles of ruler, commander, and lawgiver in addition to dispensing a "religious" teaching. This argument has been developed further by Muslim secularists to show that the combination of a dual authority, religious and political, in Muḥammad was therefore accidental and that with changed conditions, the duality should be separated. But in the Qurʾān, rules concerning political, legal, social, and other matters are not referred to Muḥammad but to God; strictly speaking, the lawgiver (*shāriʿ*) is not Muḥammad, but God.

God's right or function, then, is to command (*sharʿ,amr*), while man must accept and obey (*dīn, ṭāʿa*). It is clear that this approach, which brings all human conduct under the concept of duty or obedience to God, cannot formally distinguish between justiciable and nonjusticiable actions. For example, it is man's duty to God not to tell a lie, and it is also his duty to God—this time through man—not to steal, even though the latter is justiciable in a court of law while the former may be justiciable only at the "bar of conscience" before God. Therefore, in the overall value-structure of human conduct the primary valuation is religiomoral and, although of course humanly administered justice plays a basic role in ordering society, it is definitely secondary to the real value-order, which is the moral order. This point on the character of Islamic law has been made often,[1] but the exact implications of the relationship between law and ethics have not been fully treated. This is the central question I wish to explore.

It is well to recall that in Islam there exists a sharp distinction, even a cleavage, between law and ethics, among the users of the law if not among its producers or dispensers. The existence of *ḥiyal* literature, whose avowed purpose is to teach people how to evade law, points to a certain dislocation between morality and law. Al-Ghazālī regarded *fiqh* as "a mere science of this world" if it was not practiced with a religious attitude. He relates the following incident in the *Iḥyā*ʾ: Someone reported to Abū Ḥanīfa that his disciple, Abū Yūsuf, was resorting to the morally questionable practice of evading payment of zakat by transferring his property to his wife before it had been in his possession a whole year, as required by the law of zakat, and that his wife did the same with her property. Upon hearing this, Abū Ḥanīfa remarked, "Abū Yūsuf is a *faqīh* [as opposed to a man of religion] and, as such, he is perfectly within his rights in doing so." Al-Ghazālī condoned Abū Ḥanīfa's alleged response by insisting that law is a science of this world and therefore has nothing to do with the real science of faith, which is *ʿilm al-ākhira* (science of the hereafter).[2]

With al-Ghazālī, however, we are dealing with a mystic who is concerned with the purely spiritual aspect of human behavior. In the *Kitāb Mīzān al-ʿAmal,* for example, he observes that prayer, like dancing, contains certain physical movements and postures. If these are performed without an understanding of the true spiritual import of prayer, they are no better—and no worse—than the movements of a dancer. In the case of a dancer, at least, the movements are understandable.[3] And when al-Ghazālī and others complain about the "lawyers or *qāḍīs* of our times," it is not difficult to see what they mean. But how can one explain the allegation that Abū Ḥanīfa not only condoned but indeed was doing what a faqīh can do? Abū Ḥanīfa, we are told, was a person who refused the caliph's offer of an appointment as chief qāḍī because he was fearful of the responsibility the position entailed. Fiqh, if not the center of dīn, as al-Ghazālī would say, is certainly the bedrock of Islam. But then why should fiqh, under certain conditions, and according to al-Ghazālī probably even under normal conditions, turn out to be antagonistic to dīn?

[1] For an excellent and concise statement on this point see H. A. R. Gibb, *Mohammedanism* (Oxford: Oxford University Press, 1952), Chapter 6.

[2] *Iḥyāʾ ʿUlūm al-Dīn,* vol. 1 (Cairo: al-Maktaba al-Tijārīya al-Kubrā, n.d.), *Kitāb al-ʿIlm,* pp. 18 ff. (see also the following reference). Later, on p. 24, ll. 10 ff., al-Ghazālī, somewhat inconsistently, says that his criticism of the *fuqahā*ʾ has reference only to the later pseudo-fuqahāʾ and does not apply to the very early ones.

[3] See F. Rahman, "Theology and Law in Islam," in G. E. von Grunebaum, ed., *Theology and Law in Islam* (Wiesbaden: Otto Harassovitz, 1971), p. 93; see also al-Ghazālī's text referred to therein.

Similarly, Ibn Taimīya, some two centuries later, while discussing the execution of al-Ḥallāj, talks of fiqh or legal *ijtihād* and its relationship with the sharīʿa as well as the relationship of the Sufi inspiration of *kashf* to the sharīʿa. Ibn Taimīya complains that people often equate sharīʿa not only with law but also with the actual decisions of judges. He then states that when Sufi intuition and the ulama's ijtihād differ, then neither can claim validity but both must compete with each other for sharīʿa proofs of their respective legitimacy.[4] He does not actually define sharīʿa, but from his discussion it appears that by sharīʿa he means those norms or values or ideals that have been laid down by God, explicitly or implicitly, which are to be applied, through fiqh, to human conduct, which then must be judged against them. It is quite clear that shāriʿ (lawgiver) in this sense is God alone, and not the Prophet.

Thus there is a distinction between legal rules and an Ideal Law, and it is the latter which, strictly speaking, is the law or the Will of God. In the Qurʾān, verbal derivatives from the term "fiqh" are frequently used but they mean "understanding" of central issues preached by the Prophet and are usually equivalent to *ʿilm* (knowledge), which also always implies understanding. In only one place is fiqh used specifically for religion, in Sura 9.122, which advises Muslims that they should not all participate in wars, but that "from every segment a group should devote themselves to acquiring a deeper understanding of the Faith (*liyatafaqqahū fīʾl-dīn*) and should teach their people when they return so that these too shall receive admonition." Here "fiqh fīʾl-dīn" means "deeper understanding of the Faith," which may include rules of conduct but is certainly much more general and comprehensive. Another most important and interesting point in verse 9.122 concerns the function of the fuqahāʾ or ulama. That function is not to rule, as Khomeini contends in *Vilāyet-i Faqīh* in opposition to the Qurʾān, but to teach the community at large in order to minimize the differences between an *ʿālim* and a non-ʿālim, for the Qurʾān undoubtedly requires a community whose members are enlightened enough about Islamic teaching to be able to carry on *shūrā* (decision-making) through mutual discussion and consultation.

Despite the distinction between legal rules and the Ideal Law, a distinction supported by the Qurʾān and the later tradition—I have already mentioned al-Ghazālī and Ibn Taimīya—both fiqh and sharīʿa became generally equated with specific rules, and it is obedience to these rules that constituted the fulfillment of God's Will. Yet, as noted earlier, in Islam the paramount valuation of human conduct was moral, not legal, and decisions by judges in the courts, and even the opinions of *muftīs* or jurisconsults, did not constitute the primary manifestation of the divine will, although they were very important and were perceived, in some sense, as flowing from that

[4] F. Rahman, *Islam* (2d ed.; Chicago: University of Chicago Press, 1979), p. 113, top, quotation from Ibn Taimīya.

will. The problem, then, is: What happened to the Ideal Law or Will of God, where was it to be located, and in what actual relationship, if any, did it stand to the fiqh law?

In order to be in a position to give anything like a satisfactory answer to these questions, we should look at certain telling examples from the Qurʾān. These examples will, I think, show that whenever there are specific Qurʾānic commands and prohibitions, lawyers take them very seriously, but whenever the lawyers are faced with general Qurʾānic requirements with an ethical import, they do not know how to deal with them, and in many cases do not even try. Sura 4.2, for example, severely criticizes certain guardians of orphans for abusing the latter's property—a theme that goes back well into the Meccan period—and 4.127 states that these guardians, rather than return their property to orphan girls when they come of age, would prefer to marry them (and enjoy their property). Further, in 4.3, the Qurʾān states that if these guardians cannot do justice to the orphan girls' properties, then they may marry up to four from among the latter, provided they do justice among co-wives; but if they cannot do justice to each, they must marry only one. In 4.129, again, the Qurʾān categorically denies the possibility of justice among a plurality of wives. Now the lawyers understood 4.3 to grant a specific legal permission for marrying up to four wives; as for the justice clause, they understood it not as a specific rule but only as a general command to do justice and a recommendation to the husband's conscience. In recent times, the legislation concerning multiple marriages has been reversed in some countries; Tunisian family law, for instance, assumes that polygamy was permitted only temporarily and under certain conditions, and that the Qurʾānic command to do justice, coupled with a denial of the possibility of such justice, necessitates the prohibition of polygamy.

In 23.44, the Qurʾān gives Muslims a general command to execute freedom-purchasing contracts with their slaves, if the latter so desire, and to give such of them as are destitute a part of their own wealth. Most early fuqahāʾ maintained that this is only a recommendation, not a command, and Mālik (d. 179/795) states unequivocally that he never met an ʿālim who believed otherwise.[5] Again, in 42.32, the Qurʾān enumerates the moral characteristics of those who have faith and states that men of faith must decide their affairs by shūrā (mutual consultation), a democratic pre-Islamic Arab institution which the Qurʾān upholds. Shūrā was not developed into any institutionalized form until Muslim Modernists insisted upon a constitutional form of government in the nineteenth and twentieth centuries. It is true that the fuqahāʾ had little political power to either implement, or to cause the implementation of, shūrā, but they could at least have attempted to formulate its necessary elements, structure, and the like, something they never did.

[5] Ibid., "Epilogue," p. 298, ll. 5 ff.

The Qurʾān, from its very beginning, has been very emphatic regarding the amelioration of conditions for the poor and the deprived and has strongly advocated socioeconomic justice. In fact, these are cornerstones of the entire Qurʾānic teaching. The Qurʾān also prescribes the levying of zakat. Further, Sura 59.7, concerning the distribution of booty, defines the categories in which booty is to be divided and adds: "This is so that wealth should not circulate only among the rich ones of the society." To implement this general economic requirement it was necessary to have political power, which the fuqahāʾ lacked. They did, however, have the necessary intellectual power, and the opportunity, to explain what was meant by "circulation of wealth in the society as a whole" and to show how this could be brought about. Yet the fuqahāʾ did little to reinterpret zakat, which in any event had become a fixed law. On the question of general economic justice, we have only the disturbing opinion of the Zāhiri Ibn Ḥazm (d. 450/1058), who believed that it is an Islamic duty for the poor to revolt against the rich and against political authority if their plight is such that they are threatened with starvation. This passage of Ibn Ḥazm's[6] has been played up in recent Muslim socialist literature, but it is an isolated example and is not explicitly related to the Qurʾānic teaching on economic justice.

It is striking, indeed, how the fuqahāʾ felt either helpless before these general Qurʾānic directives or did not feel their importance strongly enough to try to explicate their legal imperatives. The fuqahāʾ did draw a distinction between *fatwā* and *taqwā,* that is, between legal imperatives and deeper moral obligations. For example, the majority of the fuqahāʾ prohibited any excess charge on a sum loaned, for that would constitute *ribā,* which the Qurʾān bans; this is fatwā, or a legal norm. But many fuqahāʾ also stated that it is unlawful, or rather, immoral for a creditor to exploit in any way the situation of the debtor vis-à-vis himself. Thus it would be reprehensible for a creditor to as much as ride on his debtor's riding beast or to take shelter from the sun in the shade of his debtor's house; this is taqwā, or a moral demand, which of course cannot be enforced through a court of law. Yet even in this example, it is both interesting and significant that instead of formulating a general principle to the effect that a creditor must not take any advantage, big or small, of anyone indebted to him, fiqh literature prefers to cite concrete examples, such as a creditor riding the debtor's beast or seeking shelter in the shade of his house.

It would be tempting to argue, as several Western writers have done, that the Arab mind is more concrete than abstract, that it works by imagination rather than by reason, and therefore can deal with particulars and minutiae better than with universals. Such theories were common in nineteenth-century

[6]See F. Rahman, "Sources and Meaning of Islamic Socialism," in Donald E. Smith, ed., *Religion and Political Modernization* (New Haven: Yale University Press, 1974), p. 256, ll. 5 ff.

Europe. I too hold that the Arab mind possesses a strong imagination and loves the concrete, but the second part of the proposition, namely, the "atomicity" of the Arab mind, to use Hamilton A. R. Gibb's phrase,[7] does not necessarily follow. In any case, not all jurists were Arab, particularly in Iraq; Abū Ḥanīfa himself was an Iranian. I think the answer must be sought in the nature of the culture, rather than in any romanticizing of ethnicity.

The Arab-Islamic culture values a living sense of moral rectitude in human conduct above everything else. Intellectualism for the sake of intellectualism—the hallmark of Greek culture and of much of modern Western culture—is perceived as a sin against human nature, if not a crime as well, for it deliberately distorts the human perspective. The nearest antecedent to Arab-Islamic culture is Syriac Christianity, which according to many Western scholars is also causally connected with it. Among the three main streams of classical Christianity, it is the Syriac which kept the Semitic moral Weltanschaung most alive. This has been adduced to explain the curious fact that the Qurʾan, in the Meccan period, hardly mentions the New Testament but refers to the Book of Moses six times as its great forerunner, despite the fact that at the time there were more Christians than Jews in and around the Arabian Peninsula. The explanation is that in Syriac Christianity, the Old Testament was given more prominence than the New Testament.

The Qurʾān is not a book of abstract ethics, but neither is it the legal document that Muslim lawyers have made it out to be. It is a work of moral admonition through and through. A large part, which deals with human relations (and which also includes many of the stories), is full of statements on the necessity of justice, fair play, goodness, kindness, forgiveness, guarding against moral peril (*ʿadl, qisṭ, iḥsān, taqwā,* and their equivalents), and so on. It is clear that these are general directives, not specific rules. But they are not abstract moral propositions either; they have a driving power, a compelling force, which abstract propositions cannot yield. This fact was acknowledged also by the Muʿtazila Rationalists, who, while insisting that "good" and "bad" (i.e., moral truth) were knowable by natural reason without the aid of Revelation, nevertheless believed that Revelation was not superfluous but helped motivate people to pursue goodness.[8]

Of course, besides certain general pronouncements made in the Qurʾān, of which we have already cited some examples and which the jurists do not appear to have taken seriously in their legislation, all the specific injunctions of the Qurʾān contain general principles as well. The jurists, at least theoretically, acknowledge that the specific injunctions of the Qurʾān are meant

[7]See H. A. R. Gibb, *Modern Trends in Islam* (Chicago: University of Chicago Press, 1946), Chapter 1, p. 6; but the entire chapter should be read.

[8]On Muʿtazila ethics and theology see the masterly treatment by George Hourani, *Islamic Rationalism* (New York: Oxford University Press, 1971).

to satisfy these general requirements or principles. They also maintain that these requirements or principles constitute the *rationes legis* (*ʿilal ʾl-aḥkām*) of the Qurʾānic injunctions. Their whole theory of *qiyās* (analogical reasoning) is based upon this premise. Thus they seek to deduce law by extricating the *ratio legis* of a certain legal text that is analagous to the case under consideration and then applying it to the given case, allowing for differences. This *ratio legis* is nothing more than a general principle which is presented as the essence of the law. In other words, it is the moral value that the law seeks to embody and realize. If values and principles were to be derived from the entire Qurʾān, it would be possible to build an ethical system that would be genuinely Qurʾānic.

If such a task had been attempted, jurists would not have been compelled to resort to principles like *istiḥsān* and *maṣlaḥa mursala,* which are specific formulations of the principle of equity and justice in general. The trouble with these principles is the difficulty of applying them well and avoiding arbitrariness. Also, these principles, as they were formulated and applied, seemed to secularize Islamic law. We are told that the function of maṣlaḥa mursala is to locate and formulate a value wherein a certain legitimate interest of the community lies but which is not connected with any sharīʿa value (aṣl sharʿī). In other words, it is in some sense definitely secular in terms of the basic nature of Islamic legislation. The case with istiḥsān (equity) is not much better. It is sometimes defined as a deviation from qiyās. This second formulation seems highly meaningful because it implies an appeal to a higher principle or value than the one upon which strict qiyās was supposed to be based. This would call for some systematization of values in terms of priorities. But this is precisely what was never done, and the two bases of legislation appeared so arbitrary that al-Shāfiʿī felt compelled to say regarding istiḥsān that whoever resorts to it claims to lay down a new sharīʿa.[9]

These three free-floating principles—maṣlaḥa, istiḥsān, and ḍarūra (necessity)—in medieval times gave the administrative authorities an instrument of great flexibility for applying sharīʿa, and afforded later rulers, particularly the Ottomans, the opportunity to systematically introduce a new state-made law that claimed to be sanctioned by sharīʿa law. The Ottoman experience, in turn, paved the way for the introduction of secular law in Turkey. Modern legal systems in Egypt and Iraq, drafted by the late Sanhūrī Pāshā, are also based on systematic appeals to the same principles of community interest and necessity without any attempt to relate them to relevant sharʿī values. Yet the same and indeed far better results could have been achieved by the juridic procedure of extracting the *rationes legis* of Qurʾānic injunctions, formulating them into general principles or values, systematizing these

[9]See n. 3; see also F. Rahman, introduction to *Islam and Modernity: Transformation of an Intellectual Tradition* (Chicago: University of Chicago Press, 1984).

principles or values, and deriving law from them. One case will illustrate the point. The Qurʾān (2.178; see also 2.92) enunciates the *lex talionis* and also confirms the system of settling a murder through blood-money (*diya*), which was practiced in pre-Islamic Arabia. This, of course, makes of murder a private crime and upon this premise rests the classical fiqh law of murder. Elsewhere, however, the Qurʾān refers to the murder of Abel by Cain and states: "For this reason, we laid it down upon the Children of Israel that whoever kills one human without his having the right to it or without there being a state of war, it is as though he has killed all mankind, and whoever gives life to one human, it is as though he has given life to all humanity . . ." (5.32), which explicitly makes the crime of murder a crime against humanity. Now a legal solution could have been derived from this general statement, but this was never done.

I am not suggesting that if the development of Qurʾānic ethics had taken place and law had been deduced from it, differences of legal opinion would have been eliminated—that would be neither possible nor desirable. But differences of opinion would have been grounded more soundly and would have been better controlled or rationalized and chaos would have been minimized. Moreover, the evolution of law could have proceeded more smoothly, the so-called "closure of the gate of ijtihād" would not have occurred and, in fact, would have become inconceivable. Resort to principles like maṣlaḥa, which were never well formulated, whose operations were uncontrolled and often arbitrary, and which were, indeed, amorphous, would have been related to sharīʿa principles. It is true that because of the lack of cohesiveness an astonishingly rich wealth of opinion on virtually all important issues has been generated along the entire legal spectrum. Abū Ḥanīfa and Mālik, for example, prohibit sharecropping and absentee landlordism; from Abū Yūsuf onward, however, most jurists allow it. In retrospect, it can be seen that between Mālik and Abū Yūsuf the differences in milieu made the crucial difference. Still, the reasoning of all three—Abū Ḥanīfa, Mālik, and Abū Yūsuf—is abstract and there is no appeal to any common principle; the differences in reasoning can be attributed to different interpretations of ḥadith. The question of birth control may serve as another example. Opinions range from outright prohibition to strong recommendation, the reasoning on both sides having no common basis; those who prohibit birth control use the necessity of strengthening the community as their main argument; others, like al-Ghazālī, say that a couple must avoid having children if they are too poor to feed them and fear that economic hardship might compel them to obtain money by unlawful means. Both sides of the issue have assumed large proportions in today's Muslim world and the division of opinion among Muslims can have grave consequences.

Perhaps the most interesting case of grave neglect of propounding theories based on sharīʿa principles is in the political field. From Morocco to Indonesia we see a continuous spectacle of personal rule (even discounting central

Asia and Afghanistan, which are under Russian occupation): monarchs, military dictators, religious autocrats, all offering themselves as the best alternative and the best form of rule for the Muslim community. The Qur'ān, as has been pointed out, gives the principle of shūrā (mutual consultation and discussion) to the Muslim community as a decision-making process, but shūrā was never developed into an institution. Instead, the caliphal form of government became, in the course of time, for Muslims and Muslim political theorists, the only valid form of rule, even though there is no word about it either in the Qur'ān or in the Prophet's sunna, except for an obviously spurious ḥadīth according to which the Prophet said, "Obey me and my rightly guided successors (*al-khulafā' al-rāshidūn*)." Since the mid-nineteenth century, practically all Modernist Muslim thinkers have contended that the only valid Muslim rule is through shūrā, which in the world of today means a representative form of government. In conformity with this ideology parliaments were instituted in several Muslim countries. But the current deluge of secular and fundamentalist dictatorships has, at least for the time being, submerged that entire democratic orientation. The curious thing is that in the Islamic dictatorships of Khomeini and Ziaul Haq, no actual reference is made either to the Qur'ān or to its shūrā principle. In fact, both men have tried to undermine that principle by insisting that the common Muslim has no sense of right and wrong, and that consequently guidance must come to him from above. Now if this argument is correct, and if the Qur'ān puts the responsibility for shūrā on the community and not on Khomeini or Ziaul Haq, then it must be concluded that the Muslim community is not in existence. Perhaps most interesting of all is the fact that while Muslim Modernists, including Shī'a thinkers like Amīr 'Alī, have insisted that Islam cannot be a theocracy since it has no priestly class, Khomeini and his colleagues are saying precisely that there is a priestly class in Islam and that it must rule; this is essentially true of Ziaul Haq's stance as well.

What lies at the bottom of this dilemma and how, if at all, can it be resolved? If I have been able to give a satisfactory answer to this question and to suggest a way towards a solution to its underlying problem, then a way will have been opened for Muslims to attain their goal, namely, a proper rediscovery of Islam—if we Muslims really wish to do so. The answer, in brief, is that the Qur'ān's message must be understood as a unity and not as so many isolated commands and injunctions. But in order to bring out the Qur'ān's message as a unity, one must start with the theology and ethics of the Qur'ān and only then approach the realm of law. The Islamic developments in history started with the law, and Muslims subsequently developed a theology that in its genesis and historical development had no connection with the law. The theology later claimed for itself the status of "crown of the sharī'a sciences" and the function of protector of the law. As Ibn Taimīya has stated, a theology which rejects the freedom and efficacy of the human will ill accords with a law that assumes human freedom and responsibility.[10] The formulation of a proper Qur'ānic theology is necessary particularly in order to define the God-man relationship. A Qur'ānic ethics was never worked out by Muslims. In the present volume, the participants at the Ninth Levi Della Vida Conference discuss the different ethical traditions that developed in Islam, some that are nearer to the Qur'ān than others, but almost none that have grown out of the Qur'ān proper. The reason, I believe, is that such an ethics presupposes a satisfactory theology. After ethics comes law, and that law must satisfy the demands of the Qur'ān as a unitary teaching.

The rise and development of Islamic law, as they actually occurred, kept the Muslims' attention focused on details, at the expense, I think, of the general requirements of the Qur'ān. It is true that the fabric of daily life is made up of details and minutiae; these can, however, be managed and properly directed, but only by recourse to ultimate principles. Whether a particular sales transaction is lawful and valid, or whether and to what extent a tailor is liable for the loss of material he had in his possession, are examples of the problems men face throughout their lives. Unless there is a mechanism for defining the nature of human responsibility and for applying the concepts of justice, fair play, kindness, and mercy to *all* the data of actual life—concepts which the Qur'ān emphasizes so untiringly—the law cannot really provide the necessary foundation for "the good life" envisaged by the great jurists. Eventually law must run the risk of a critique such as that of al-Ghazālī, quoted earlier.

In the absence of a living link with ultimate principles, it became necessary, through the second century in particular, to invoke the infallible authority of the Prophet—*Prophetus ex machina,* as it were—and attribute to him all the trivia of daily life. The minutiae of law were spun out as isolated items of legislation, with the Ḥanafis invoking "considered opinion (*ra'y*)" or "analogical reasoning (qiyās)," and the Mālikis relying on "the practice of Madina" (*ʿamal ahl al-Madīna*). In the absence of any substantive unifying principles that could bind these isolated items into a system, the need for an infallible authority is understandable.

What was needed was the development of ijtihād and ijmāʿ in constant interaction with each other. Ijtihād was needed not only for a horizontal deduction of law as it was actually used, but also for a vertical development of arching and overarching general principles in order to progressively subsume the multiplicity of principles under them. Later jurists like al-Shāṭibī (d. 1388 C.E.) and Ibn Rushd (d. 1198 C.E.) worked on the general principles of the sharīʿa from different points of view, but this was a somewhat different exercise. Al-Shāṭibī and ʿIzz al-Dīn ibn ʿAbd al-Salām al-

[10] Rahman, *Islam,* p. 113.

Sulamī (d. 1182 C.E.) aimed at extracting the purpose of the laws (*aghrāḍ al sharīʿa* or *al-maṣāliḥ*). Ibn Rushd tried to clarify the basis and methodology of different schools of law and to explain their divergence, particularly between the Ḥanafīs and the Mālikis, a task to which he brought a cogency and a lucidity which only philosophical training could have given him. Al-Shāṭibī is fully aware that isolated sharīʿa proofs, like individual verses of the Qurʾān or ḥadīths (even if the latter are *mutawātir,* i.e., handed down by an overwhelming number of transmitters), cannot constitute sharīʿa proofs properly speaking and cannot reach the point of certainty, unless such proofs, of different provenance, converge upon one specific point (*taḍāfur al-adilla*).[11] Although al-Shāṭibī, so far as I can read him, is talking about individual points to be proved, for example, the obligation of prayers, his argument definitely has the potentiality of being applicable to Islam as a whole, or to the message of the Qurʾān as a whole. This would necessarily entail not only a horizontal movement but a vertical movement as well. The famous maxim quoted by many lawyers and numerous commentators on the Qurʾān, which states that "parts of the Qurʾān are mutually explanatory (*al-Qurʾān yufassiru baʿḍuhū baʿḍan*)," also implies that the Qurʾān is a unity and not a jumble of isolated or mutually contradictory ideas.

Ethics may be defined as a theory of moral right and wrong. This is exactly what the Qurʾān claims to do; for this is what guidance (hudā) means. In this definition, the terms "theory" and "moral right and wrong" are basic. Some might argue that the two concepts are incompatible because moral right and wrong are practical and, as such, have to be intuited rather than theorized, and that the more one theorizes about right and wrong, the more one recedes from a real sense of what they are. I suspect that this type of consideration was, perhaps unconsciously, working among Muslims. In fact, I suspect that it was at work in the Semitic culture alluded to earlier, which manifests a sort of instinctive abhorrence of general abstract propositions, particularly in the moral field, which in that culture constitutes the primary field of human endeavor. Morality is not expressed in terms of propositions but rather in terms of divine dictates and actions. On this view, right and wrong, which are primarily qualities of actions, cannot be determined by an appeal to general propositions but only with reference to the state of mind called taqwā or the living sense of God's presence. There is, no doubt, a point here and one can even say that the more ethical theorization there has been in modern times, the less concern there has been about actual right and wrong. This was the crux of the difference between the Muʿtazila and their opponents, the Ashʿarites, who believed that right and wrong originate in the divine imperative rather than in rational propositions, and that "good" and "bad" are known through Revelation rather than

[11] Rahman, *Islam and Modernity,* pp. 21–22.

through Reason (although, as I pointed out earlier, the Muᶜtazila did admit that Revelation has a motive power which Reason does not possess, at least not sufficiently).

This is why I stress the need for a system of ethics that grows out of the Qurʾān. I do not say that Greek ethics or Persian ethics or, indeed, modern ethical theories are necessarily antagonistic to the Qurʾān, but for Muslims there are multiple reasons why a Qurʾānic ethics must be worked out. First of all, Muslims believe that the Qurʾān is the Word of God. Second, they believe that the Qurʾān contains, actually or potentially, the answers to all the questions of everyday life. Since the questions are infinite, the Qurʾān must contain the answers potentially. To get actual answers requires the exercise of mind and spirit. There is a profound statement on this subject attributed by the Shīᶜa tradition to ᶜAlī: "The Qurʾān speaks (only) if you ask it to speak," that is, you ask sincerely;[12] this is ijtihād. But if one uses ijtihād to elicit trivial details from the Qurʾān, one will feel the need for some validating authority, and this is why, as I have stated, at a certain stage of the development of fiqh, the need for Prophetic authority was felt and then satisfied by the fabrication of ḥadīth. The early Ḥanafīs were able to a large extent to avoid this drastic solution by their stated position—which remained effective even after al-Shāfiᶜīs wholesale introduction of ḥadīth into law—that in the presence of a definite principle derived from the Qurʾān (*aṣl qaṭᶜī*), they would reject a ḥadīth if it was in conflict with either. What is this aṣl qaṭᶜī, or definite principle derived from Revelation? It is none other than what I previously described as the *ratio legis,* or generalized statement. This is the beginning of the vertical movement or discovery of the more general principle. Such a principle needs no authentication of its details by a ḥadīth report because it is more reliable than most ḥadīths, and certainly the *akhbār al-āḥād* (i.e., ḥadīths transmitted in a single chain), which, in fact, constitute the majority of ḥadīths in the sphere of law.

If the argument thus far is correct, then the term uṣūl al-fiqh is better applied to the general precepts and principles that are either explicitly formulated in the Qurʾān or are explicable from its *rationes legis,* than to the celebrated "four roots of law," namely, the Qurʾān, the sunna, ijtihād, and ijmāᶜ or consensus. For, on the view that we have tried to expound, uṣūl al-fiqh, or principles of law, is that body of ethical teaching which will have emerged as a result of a systematic formulation of the *rationes legis* or objectives of the Qurʾānic legislation and injunctions. The Qurʾān and the authentic sunna of the Prophet are the *material sources of law,* while ijtihād and ijmāᶜ are the *methodology of Islamic theology, ethics, and law.* Through this methodology, what is to be worked out in the first instance

[12]See *K. al-Kāfī,* vol. 1 (Tehran: al-Ṣadūq Press, 1381/1961), p. 61, l. 7; for the saying attributed to Jaᶜfar al-Ṣādiq, see also p. 59, ll. 7 ff.

is the theology, and then the value-structure or higher objectives and goals of the Qurʾān: What kind of man does the Qurʾān desire to mold and, granted such individuals, what kind of sociopolitical order does it want to establish on earth?

In classical Islamic law, because ultimate values were not distinguished from instrumental ones, a good deal of confusion arose regarding the nature of laws of different provenance. It is certain, for example, that the Qurʾān views the establishment of a Muslim community as essential for its task and will not be content with good individuals only; further, this community is charged with the task of establishing a sociopolitical order. The community is thus the necessary instrument for this purpose. Later, not only was the community declared inerrant, most probably through considerations of the infallibility of ijmāʿ, but, in law it came to be regarded as something ultimate. A person's decision to abjure the community or the Islamic faith, for example, was made a capital crime. The Qurʾān states: "Those who believed, then disbelieved, again believed and once again disbelieved and then became entrenched in disbelief, God will not pardon them nor show them a right way" (4.137; cf. 3.90). In 2.256 the Qurʾān clearly formulates the principle of freedom of faith: "There can be no coercion in matters of faith—truth has become clear from falsehood." This is a good illustration of the conflict between the values and principles laid down by the Qurʾān and those deduced by the jurists on the basis of the logic of the Islamic Imperium, which emerged by swift conquests shortly after the Prophet's death. Before the conquests, however, immediately on hearing the news of the Prophet's death, many Arab tribes rebelled against the political authority of Medina and reverted to their old tribal sovereignty. They did not abjure Islam—although Muslim historians and lawyers have called the reaction by the misnomer "apostasy movement"—but insisted that they would pay taxes not to the central authority at Medina but to their own tribal organizations. Otherwise they would carry out all the duties devolving upon a Muslim, like prayer, fasting, pilgrimage, and so on. This shows clearly that theirs was a political rebellion. The rebellion was put down by force of arms, but by a mistaken argument Muslim lawyers deduced from this that a person who leaves the faith of Islam deserves capital punishment. The clearly stated Qurʾānic verse 4.137, quoted above, was ignored. Hence the source of the Islamic law on apostasy is not the Qurʾān but the logic of the Islamic Imperium. The science of Qurʾānic ethics will have to decide the relative place of both in the structure of Islam.

# ETHICS AND CLASSICAL ISLAMIC PHILOSOPHY: A STUDY OF AVERROES' *COMMENTARY ON PLATO'S REPUBLIC*

CHARLES E. BUTTERWORTH
University of Maryland

## Introduction

There is more emphasis in classical Islamic philosophy on virtue than on ethics. For Farabi and Averroes, and also to some extent for Avicenna, ethics is a part of virtue. Of the four kinds or parts of human excellence—theoretical virtue, deliberative virtue, moral virtue, and proficiency or skill in the practical arts—ethics pertains only to one, moral virtue. Moral virtue is investigated by a Farabi or an Averroes more to determine what it comprises and what end it serves than to explain how it might be acquired. The habitual actions we perform in order to develop the virtue of courage or moderation fall within the realm of ethics. Precisely because there are no such actions we might practice in order to develop the virtue of wisdom or justice, each being, instead, dependent on excellent discernment, ethics has nothing to do with them.[1] Moreover, since ethics is limited to the actions performed so as to acquire the virtues in question, to the exercises, as it

[1] See Farabi, *The Attainment of Happiness*, in *Alfarabi's Philosophy of Plato and Aristotle*, trans. Muhsin Mahdi (Glencoe: The Free Press, 1962), sections 2, 17–18, 26, and 29; and *Averroes on Plato's "Republic,"* trans. Ralph Lerner (Ithaca: Cornell University Press, 1974), 22:9–12. The page and line references are to the edition of the Hebrew text, the Arabic not being extant; see *Averroes' Commentary on Plato's "Republic,"* ed. and trans. E. I. J. Rosenthal (Cambridge: Cambridge University Press, 1956). Unless otherwise indicated, I rely upon Lerner's re-edition and retranslation of the text. Though he differs from Rosenthal in basing his translation on the oldest Hebrew manuscript as well as in the approach he takes to translation and interpretation (see Preface, pp. ii–ix, and Appendix II, pp. 159–162), Lerner preserves the pages and line numbers of Rosenthal's Hebrew edition in the left-hand margins of his work. Despite a few disagreements with Lerner about particular readings, translations, and paragraph divisions, I consider his translation and edition to be excellent; see my "On Sigmund's 'Review of Ralph Lerner's *Averroes on Plato's Republic*'," *Political Theory*, 4 (1976), 505–506.

were, by which we come to be courageous, moderate, or virtuous in any number of ways, ethics is not the same as virtue. It is, rather, the instrument of virtue.

That ethics—that is, the moral habits and character traits by which the various moral virtues are acquired—is viewed in such a restricted manner has consequences for the political teaching of Farabi and Averroes. Considering ethics to be no more than a means whereby the citizens of a virtuous religious community or well-ordered city may be trained to act so as to further their ultimate happiness, both of these thinkers concentrate on the broader issue of what makes such a community virtuous or on the nature of ultimate happiness. Differently stated, they deem it more important to inquire into the end of civic association than into the means by which it is achieved.

A similar focus characterizes classical Greek philosophy, especially that of Plato and Aristotle. In dialogues like the *Protagoras* and *Meno,* Socrates is intent above all on determining what virtue is and whether it is teachable; considerations of how to acquire it arise only incidentally as illustrations or arguments ancillary to the major investigation. Even in the *Republic,* his primary goal is to arrive at a proper understanding of what justice is and why it is good; the education of the guardians in courage, moderation, and eventually the idea of the good is set forth only so that Socrates may illustrate the goodness of justice in the city, his premise being that it is easier to see how justice functions in a large entity than in something as small as a human soul. At the end of Book One and the beginning of Book Two of the *Nicomachean Ethics,* Aristotle provides the grounds for the restrictive understanding of ethics which Farabi and Averroes later make their own. Aristotle's goal being to investigate human happiness, something he takes to be an activity of the soul directed towards virtue (I.xiii.1102$^{a}$5), he briefly examines its make-up and contents himself with the generally accepted account that it is divided into a rational and irrational part, the latter being further subdivided into a part which, though irrational, participates in reason or is mindful of it, and a part which does not (I.xiii.1102$^{a}$29–30 and 1102$^{b}$12–29). The virtues or excellences appropriate to the rational part of the soul—wisdom or prudence—are called intellectual or theoretical virtues, whereas those proper to the reason-heeding irrational part of the soul—liberality or moderation—are called moral virtues (I.xiii.1103$^{a}$4–6). Yet one could just as accurately call this latter kind ethical virtue, for the Greek (*aretē ēthikē*) in fact admits of such a translation. And Aristotle suggests that it might be so named because it is acquired by habit (*ethos*) rather than by instruction, as is the case with intellectual virtue (II.i.1103$^{a}$14–18). Having made these distinctions, he turns to a detailed examination of the various moral and intellectual virtues and of their constituents.

Virtue or, more precisely, the inquiry into virtue must be emphasized as long as the human good is not known. The condition for ethical conduct—that is, performing the actions that lead to the acquisition of the moral virtues—being sufficient is that we believe it to be the major part of human happiness, that we are content with what common opinion says about happiness and its acquisition. Such belief or commitment is not consonant with strict virtuous conduct, for the latter demands that we know why we perform good actions and that we choose to perform them. To satisfy either criterion, we must undertake for ourselves the inquiry into the nature of the good.

Virtue in all of its aspects receives primary attention in classical Greek and Islamic philosophy for yet another reason. It sets the standard by which to determine the soundness of political regimes and rank them. This is evident in Plato's *Republic* insofar as the city in speech, sometimes referred to by Socrates as the true and beautiful city, stands out as something against which all other political communities can be measured. Aristotle's ranking of the different kinds of regimes in the *Politics* according to the virtue of the ruler or rulers is similar. In the *Attainment of Happiness,* in the *Book of Religion,* and the *Political Regime,* Farabi distinguishes between good and bad rulers on the basis of the virtuous or vicious ends to which they aspire. Above all, such an emphasis on virtue is evident in Averroes' *Commentary on Plato's Republic.* As will become evident in the subsequent discussion, Averroes organizes this commentary so as to explain that all of the virtues must be provided for in a well-ordered community and, taking his bearings from Farabi as well as from an unconventional understanding of Plato and Aristotle, that their proper realization depends upon the primacy of wisdom being secured.

## An Overview of Averroes' *Commentary*

At the end of his *Middle Commentary on Aristotle's Nicomachean Ethics,* Averroes speaks of Aristotle's *Politics* with some awareness of the arguments it contains against Plato's *Republic.* He then goes on to explain that the relationship between the *Nicomachean Ethics* and the *Politics* or the *Republic* with respect to politics is the same as that between the general and the particular parts of the art of medicine.[2] Just as the first or general part of the art of medicine provides an account of health and sickness, so the first part of politics identifies and explains the habits and actions which establish the sound order of the human soul and eventually of the political community.

[2]See Averroes, *In libros decem Moralium Nicomachiorum expositio,* in *Aristotelis opera cum Averrois commentariis* (Venice: apud Junctas, 1562; repr. ed., Frankfurt: Minerva, 1962), vol. 3, folio 160 G–L. As is well known, the opinion that the *Nicomachean Ethics* leads to the *Politics* is based on the last paragraph of the former work (X.ix.1181$^{b}$16–23). Recently, however, Carnes Lord has argued persuasively that these lines are not by Aristotle and do not refer to his *Politics.* Part of Lord's argument is based on his contention that all of the relevant references in the *Politics* are to Aristotle's *Eudemian Ethics,* not to his *Nicomachean Ethics;* see Carnes Lord, "The Character and Composition of Aristotle's *Politics,*" *Political Theory,* 9 (1981), 472–474.

If this general part can be called the theoretical or scientific part, and if medicine and politics ultimately aim at some kind of precise activity, then each must also admit of a more specific part. Indeed, taking up the same analogy in the opening lines of his *Commentary on Plato's Republic,* Averroes observes that the parallel in politics to the account offered in the second or practical part of medicine about the way health may be brought about and sickness eradicated is the explanation of how to establish or improve the habits and actions which make the individual soul or the community sound, as well as how to remove those habits and actions which interfere with such soundness (21:19–22:5).

Incidentally, this analogy should not be understood as invalidating the distinction between ethics and virtue made in the previous section. Plato's *Republic* is no more a handbook on ethics than is Aristotle's *Politics,* and Averroes' *Commentary on Plato's Republic* is certainly not a step-by-step account of how to bring the various virtues into being. To the contrary, Averroes uses this analogy to argue that the emphasis in the second part of politics is on practice or action, a point to which he returns frequently in the course of his commentary. The earlier distinction remains inviolate: Ethics is an instrument for securing moral virtue, which is itself only one part of virtue. In Plato's *Republic,* as in Averroes' *Commentary on Plato's Republic,* the virtues are investigated to determine both what they are and how they affect political life.

Despite what he knows of Aristotle's disagreements in the *Politics* with Plato's *Republic,* Averroes has no qualms about linking the two works in this fashion. In fact, as he explains at the beginning of his *Commentary on Plato's Republic,* the similarity between the two works is such that he was prompted to comment on Plato's *Republic* simply because Aristotle's *Politics* had not reached him. It would seem, then, that the two works are interchangeable for all practical purposes. However, there is a missing element in this analogy between politics and medicine: Whereas Aristotle's *Politics* or Plato's *Republic* represents the practical or particular part and Aristotle's *Nicomachean Ethics* the theoretical or general, no mention is made of a corresponding theoretical work by Plato. Yet had Averroes paired the *Republic* with the *Nicomachean Ethics,* he could then have paired the *Laws* with the *Politics.*[3] And such a pairing would have more accurately captured the basic features of all four works. Moreover, the analogy is weakened by another anomaly. In the course of his commentary, Averroes makes it quite apparent that even though he is extremely familiar with Aristotle's

[3]For another instance of an incomplete juxtaposition between the writings of Plato and Aristotle on politics, but with Aristotle not receiving his due in this case, see Avicenna, *Fī Aqsām al-ʿUlūm al-ʿAqlīyah* in *Tisʿ Rasāʾil* (Cairo, 1908), 107:15–108:3; an English translation of this may be found in *Medieval Political Philosophy: A Sourcebook,* ed. Ralph Lerner and Muhsin Mahdi (Glencoe: The Free Press, 1963), p. 97.

*Nicomachean Ethics,* he has not yet commented upon it.[4] Conversely, at the end of his *Middle Commentary* on that treatise, after explaining the way it represents the first part of politics and the *Politics* or *Republic* the second, lamenting that the *Politics* has not reached the people of his peninsula, and alluding to Aristotle's criticisms of the *Republic* as well as making precise criticisms of his own, he says absolutely nothing about having already commented on it.

In effect, Averroes chooses to ignore the usual distinctions made between Aristotelian and Platonic works as well as those concerning the prior and posterior relationship between the first and second parts of politics. Such a tactic permits him to introduce reflections on the *Nicomachean Ethics* at different points in the course of his explanation of the *Republic* and thus to create the impression that there is basic philosophic agreement between Plato and Aristotle, a position that would be very difficult to advance were the *Republic* to be read in the manner suggested above. In addition, by substituting arguments from the *Nicomachean Ethics* for certain passages of the *Republic,* Averroes is able to arrive at a novel interpretation of both works. Above all, this manner of interpreting Plato's *Republic* allows Averroes to take as a practical suggestion for statecraft something which Socrates himself characterizes as a paradigm set up in heaven and which his young interlocutor Glaucon understands to be simply a city in speech.[5]

Averroes divides his commentary into three treatises, each corresponding to particular books of Plato's dialogue. The first treatise corresponds to the first five books of the *Republic.* However, alleging that he is interested only in the scientific arguments to be found in the dialogue and not in the dialectical ones (21:3–4; see also 105:26–27), Averroes does not comment on the discussions which take place in Book One and the first half of Book Two. In their place is a summary treatment of the virtues and their relationship to decent political life highly reminiscent of Books One, Six, and Ten of the *Nicomachean Ethics* and the first part of Farabi's *Attainment of Happiness* (22:6–23:15, 23:18–30, and 24:10–25:9). Ostensibly, the second treatise corresponds to Books Six and Seven of the *Republic.* In reality, Averroes replaces Socrates' similes about the idea of the good with an account of theoretical knowledge drawn primarily from Aristotelian premises and pushes Aristotle's arguments in Book Six of the *Nicomachean Ethics* to conclusions which conflict with our traditional thinking about Aristotle (64:28–74:12). The third treatise corresponds in a superficial manner to

[4] See Averroes, *Commentary on Plato's Republic,* 22:9–12, 65:8–9, 87:10–12, and 102:30–31 with 61:17–18.

[5] *Republic* IX, 592A–B. Though Averroes also acknowledges subsequently that this city is one "that we have described in speech" (64:26–27), he certainly does not mean thereby that it can exist only in speech (see 44:28–29 and 45:13–14).

Books Eight and Nine of the *Republic.* It also contains a long introductory discussion of the different kinds of imperfect regimes which closely resembles Farabi's discussion of the same topic in the *Political Regime* (80:17–87:12). Nothing more than a brief statement about the general theme of Book Ten of the *Republic* is provided, for Averroes contends that the discussion there —like that in Book One and the first half of Book Two—is basically dialectical (105:11–25, esp. 105:14).

By treating the *Republic* as he does, that is, by claiming that he will abstract all the scientific arguments from the text and leave the dialectical arguments aside, Averroes approaches it in the same manner as he usually does works by Aristotle.[6] Now it is clear from the two instances mentioned in the preceding paragraph and from yet others that Averroes does try to minimize the fundamental differences between Plato's and Aristotle's teachings. Still, it is one thing to create the impression that Plato and Aristotle are ultimately in basic agreement and quite another to urge that there is no reason to read or explain a Platonic dialogue any differently than one does an Aristotelian treatise. Owing to his Aristotelian reading of the *Republic,* Averroes' account contains no reference to the setting of the dialogue, that is, to the time, place, or circumstances in which the discussion about justice occurs. Nor does he make any attempt to speak about the different characters who participate in the dialogue. He says nothing, for example, about Polemarchus' aggressiveness, Thrasymachus' transformation from an enraged opponent of Socrates to a charmed and eager participant in the discussion, Glaucon's tenacity and general lustfulness, or Adeimantus' gentleness. He does not pause to consider what is sound and unsound in the different definitions of justice set forth by Cephalus, Polemarchus, and Thrasymachus in the first book of the *Republic.*[7] Above all, he passes over in silence the whole question of the founding of the first city and the doubts expressed by Socrates about whether or not this is the true and healthy city.[8]

Attention to these dramatic features—the setting of the dialogue, character of the interlocuters, and various by-ways of the discussion—is called for because of Plato's allusions to the dangers and difficulties of writing about philosophical problems.[9] To understand his dialogues the reader needs to reflect on what might have been, as well as on what actually was, said or done and on the circumstances surrounding such speech or action, as does anyone who seeks to understand a conversation. Arguments in dialogues, as in conversations, are addressed to particular persons and must be considered

[6]See Averroes, *Kitāb al-Samāʿ al-Ṭabīʿī,* in *Rasāʾil Ibn Rushd* (Hyderabad: Maṭbaʿah Dāʾirat al-Maʿārif al-ʿUthmānīyah, 1947), 2:4–3:7, and *Kitāb Mā Baʿd al-Ṭabīʿah,* ed. ʿUthmān Amīn (Cairo: Muṣṭafā al-Bābī al-Ḥalabī, 1958), 1:5–6.

[7]See, however, Averroes, *Commentary on Plato's Republic,* 47:29–48:2.

[8]*Republic* II, 369B–372E.

[9]See Plato, *Epistle* VII, 341B–345C; also *Phaedrus* 270C–272E and 274E–278E.

from the perspective of their immediate context. In dialogues—which are, after all, extended conversations—the context offers clues about the quality of the argument, the status of the larger question to whose solution the dialogue is devoted, and the real or nonconversational position of Plato or Socrates. In sum, before Plato's dialogues can be explained as treatises, that is, as expositions of a theme, they must first be understood for what they are.

Still, the goal here is not to explain how a Platonic dialogue should be read, but to emphasize what Averroes misses by reading the *Republic* in this particular way. And that issue is raised only in order to try to fathom why he does so. Assuming that he did know it was a dialogue, at least three reasons come to mind. First, he claims to have discovered one place in the *Republic* where Plato himself turned away from the dialectical approach in order to set forth a demonstrative argument (103:16–105:3, esp. 104:9–11). It could be said, then, that Averroes is only following Plato's example and applying that rule to the whole dialogue.

A second reason is the one Averroes adduces for following this procedure in his commentaries on Aristotelian texts. Here, as elsewhere, he expresses the opinion that the sciences have been completed in his time (63:1–3).[10] According to this position, dialectic is useful only so long as there is a need to investigate these basic problems. Now that they have been resolved, it is useful only as an exercise or as a tool for instruction. Based on generally accepted opinions and leading only to conclusions of the same order, dialectical arguments are inferior to demonstrative ones. After all, demonstrative arguments move from premises that are certain to equally certain and even universally valid conclusions. Even though Averroes acknowledges that dialectical arguments have more intellectual rigor and lead to something more substantial than the persuasive kinds of imitations achieved by rhetorical and poetical arguments, he neither considers dialectic suitable for pursuing scientific truths nor accords it the same rank as does Plato's Socrates (29:23–26). Thus by refusing to discuss the dialectical arguments of the *Republic,* Averroes intimates that his commentary has the status of a theoretical work which relies on demonstrative reasoning. Now given his equally explicit emphasis here on the fundamental differences between theoretical and practical science (21:8–18), this conjecture may seem unwarranted. Yet when his treatment of dialectic in this commentary is contrasted with the place he accords that art in his *Middle Commentary on Aristotle's Topics,* it is difficult to deny its plausibility.

In that commentary, Averroes makes three major departures from Aristotle's text in order to emphasize the importance of dialectic for philosophical investigation into the theoretical sciences and for understanding the

[10]See *Kitāb al-Samāᶜ al-Ṭabīᶜī,* 3:1–7, and also "General Introduction," par. 1, in my forthcoming edition and translation of Averroes' *Short Commentaries on Aristotle's Logic.*

practical sciences. (a) When commenting on Aristotle's remarks about the usefulness of dialectic with respect to philosophy and the theoretical sciences, he goes beyond Aristotle's text to illustrate how it can be employed to distinguish between true and false premises in physics, metaphysics, or political science. He notes, however, that despite the similar usefulness of dialectic with respect to the practical arts, it has no such value for the mathematical sciences. Then, to make this point utterly persuasive, Averroes asserts that Aristotle almost never used demonstrative arguments in physics, metaphysics, or political science without first using dialectic to test his arguments. Averroes also stresses the merits of dialectic for discerning whether an argument has been stated correctly and for getting at the principles of an art, but only insofar as those principles are generally accepted. Citing Aristotle's procedure in *De Interpretatione* as an illustration of the latter case, he adds that dialectic can be equally useful with either practical or particular arts.[11] (b) Later, when commenting on Aristotle's remarks about which dialectical problems ought to be examined and which not, Averroes contends that problems arising in theoretical sciences, practical sciences, or logic can be investigated by means of dialectic, but that in such investigations one should always strive either to help the multitude or to further philosophy.[12] (c) Finally, when commenting on Aristotle's remarks about how dialectical propositions may be secured, he says nothing about the distinction Aristotle draws between dialectic and philosophy.[13] When his silence about Aristotle's statement of this difference is compared with his explicit attempts to stretch Aristotle's other remarks about the philosophical uses of dialectic, it appears that Averroes seeks to characterize dialectic as useful for philosophical or theoretical investigation and for the practical sciences. Such a characterization of dialectic moves the art closer to the understanding Plato's Socrates held of it and away from Aristotle's. Yet when he discusses the art of dialectic in his *Commentary on Plato's Republic,* Averroes does the opposite:

[11]See Averroes, *Talkhīṣ Kitāb al-Jadal,* ed. Charles E. Butterworth and Ahmad Haridi (Cairo: General Egyptian Book Organization, 1979), pars. 5–7, with Aristotle, *Topics* 101$^{a}$34–101$^{b}$4. Elsewhere Averroes argues that it is not possible for the practitioner of an art to derive the principles of the art from the art itself, unless these principles are self-evident. Thus, not even demonstrative speculative arts can derive their principles from demonstrative speculative arts alone; they also need to use practical arts. Curiously, he does not mention in this context the merits of dialectic for such an investigation; see "Book of Demonstration," par. 80, in *Short Commentaries on Aristotle's Logic.*

The reference to Aristotle's *De Interpretatione* is to 16$^{a}$20–16$^{b}$34. For Averroes' explanation of this passage, see *Talkhīṣ Kitāb al-ʿIbārah,* ed. Mahmoud Kassem, Charles E. Butterworth, and Ahmad Haridi (Cairo: General Egyptian Book Organization, 1981), or *Averroes' Middle Commentaries on Aristotle's Categories and De Interpretatione,* trans. Charles E. Butterworth (Princeton: Princeton University Press, 1983), pars. 4–14.

[12]See Averroes, *Talkhīṣ Kitāb al-Jadal,* par. 23, with Aristotle, *Topics* 105$^{a}$3–9.

[13]See ibid., par. 29, with Aristotle, *Topics* 105$^{a}$34–105$^{b}$38.

He so characterizes dialectic that it more closely resembles Aristotle's understanding than that of Plato's Socrates.

Thus, by claiming to leave dialectical arguments aside in his consideration of Plato's *Republic* and otherwise attempting to denigrate the intellectual merit of dialectic, Averroes seeks to present his commentary as being similar to a scientific treatise. He pretends to use demonstrative arguments to discuss a practical art—the all-important art of governing cities—in order to persuade his reader that his reflections about practical matters are guided by theoretical science. I would argue further that he seeks to do so, even though he has recourse to dialectical arguments in the treatise, because part of his goal here is to go beyond a mere explanation of Plato's *Republic* and to draw the outlines of his own city in speech. For the most part Averroes has recourse to dialectical arguments in order to express popular opinions he wishes to refute or to capture the essence of a possible objection to one of his arguments, but on some occasions he utilizes dialectical arguments to advance his own teaching (65:29–67:3, 70:3–14, 71:11–20, 73:25–74:12, and 85:15–21). He alerts the reader to his own legislative design in this treatise by the frequent contrasts he draws between "these cities" and "this city," as in "these cities in this time of ours" and "this city that we are involved in bringing forth,"[14] as well as by his explicit endorsements of certain features of Plato's city in speech—for example, the poverty of the guardians, the community of women and children as well as the regulations pertaining to sexual intercourse, and the rule of philosophy. The city Averroes is intent upon bringing about will be not one but many virtuous cities or communities, each one adapted to the particular conditions of the different major climates and the different kinds of human beings or the different regions of the world (46:14–19).

The third reason for Averroes' leaving the dialectical arguments of the *Republic* aside is related. He seems to be less interested in pursuing the arguments about justice as they are developed in the *Republic* than in setting forth his own teaching about the relationship between theory and practice. Seizing upon Socrates' characterization of justice as that which establishes a basic harmony between the different parts of the soul or of the city, Averroes defines justice at the very beginning of the commentary (23:31–33) and then

[14]References by Averroes to what happens "among us" or "in this time of ours" abound, as do references to "that city which we are describing in speech" or to "this virtuous city." None of these poses any problem. Nor do most of Averroes' references to "this city," for it is generally evident that by "this city" he means the city he is describing in speech, the city originally sketched out in speech by Socrates. But when Averroes speaks of "these cities" it is not always immediately evident to which cities he is referring—those of his own day or those other cities which might exist in contrast to the virtuous city. As nearly as I can tell, he uses the term "these cities" 55 times; in 35 (or about 63%) of those instances, the reference is to the cities of his day and is always negative.

drops the issue.[15] For him to pay any closer attention to the argument about justice in the *Republic* would turn him aside from his own task of substituting a modified Aristotelian view of the different kinds of human virtues and of the relationship among these virtues as well as between the virtues and the practical arts for the account provided by Socrates. Even though he ends up in substantial agreement with Socrates about the need for practice to be guided by theory, he arrives at this conclusion by a unique line of reasoning. Adopting Aristotle's identification of politics or the art of governing cities as the art of arts, Averroes reworks Aristotle's basic teaching to show why this art of arts must depend upon theoretical wisdom for its direction.

Clearly, the second and third reasons are the most interesting. Averroes indicates his legislative intentions not only by embracing Plato's recommendations about such matters as the guardians being forbidden to have personal property and marriage being a communal arrangement, but also by criticizing many of the practices actually occurring in his own or in other Muslim regimes. Thus, not content simply to report on Plato's charges against Homer and the poets of his day, Averroes extends the criticism to include the shortcomings of the Arab poets and the errors of the dialectical theologians (32:23–24, 33:3, 34:13–14, 30:26–31:15, and 66:22–67:3). At a level somewhat more removed, he likewise bewails the multiplicity of sophists and would-be philosophers who have gained undue power (64:9–15, 70:12–14, and 77:28–29). In addition, he finds music—especially melodies intended to bring about a receptiveness to virtue in those listening—to have become corrupt in his time (35:11–12) and the daily diet to be the cause of much sickness (37:15–19). Moreover, Averroes is dismayed both that some arts have become useless because they are pursued by too many individuals (43:31–44:5) and that the critics of his day are so perverse as to assign ranks of honor on the basis of financial achievement (50:21–51:2). Finally, he berates his fellow citizens for the role they ascribe to women and points to the evils such a policy engenders (54:6–13). In this regard, Averroes contrasts the provisions for sexual unions sketched out in the *Republic* with those prevalent in his own time and applauds the positive features of the former (55:9–12 and 57:30–58:14).

Apart from drawing attention to these views by contrasting what is said in the *Republic* with what is current in his own time, Averroes intimates that he endorses these opinions by speaking in his own name or by speaking as though to a specific addressee. He usually distinguishes his opinions from those of Plato by juxtaposing "we say" to "he said," but occasionally he

[15] I am, of course, aware of the subsequent discussion of justice (*Commentary on Plato's Republic*, 50:10–52:29), but my point is that this discussion in no way modifies the earlier, hastily adopted definition.

stresses certain points by declaring "I say" or "we ourselves say." Of the twenty-six times that he uses the second person singular, on twenty-one occasions—or almost 81 percent of the time—he does so in order to make arguments comprehensible only to someone familiar with philosophy as well as with Arabic culture and the detailed history of his own regime. And two of these references (105:4–10 and 27–28) can be only to the ruling monarch.

The latter characteristic may account for the imprecision which marks both Averroes' description of the regimes existing in his region at this particular time and his account of the different kinds of law, including divine law. When trying to explain the different stages of corruption which lead from the best regime to tyrannical rule, he repeatedly refers to what one familiar with the cities of his time and region might discern. The issue is not their badness per se, but the kind of badness which afflicts them. At times he intimates that these regimes suffer from the ills of democracy and are about to or actually have become tyrannies (84:19–22, 96:23–26, 98:3–4, and 101:16–18), while at other times he describes them as stricken by the avarice characteristic of oligarchy (93:10–11) and as still carrying the symptoms of timocratic rule (89:31, 92:4–8, and 103:8–12). Similarly, despite numerous references throughout the commentary to the various kinds of law, including divine law, he never clearly distinguishes between them. Human law, which seems to be something like basic natural law, is distinct from both conventional law or nomos and divine law. Even though the nomos is man-made law, it is not simply subordinate to both natural and divine law. Moreover, it is especially difficult to determine how human and divine law stand in relation to each other hierarchically.

From this perspective of a general overview of the work, it is difficult to explain such anomalies. Everything mentioned thus far merely points to the inescapable conclusion that Averroes considers a fundamental political transformation to be the only way to meet the manifold problems of his day. His criticisms of existing practices, his endorsements of Plato's admittedly far-reaching recommendations, and his remarks about the relationship between nomos, human law, and divine law all indicate that the new polity he would like to bring into being is not completely consonant with the dominant opinion in his time and region, not to mention the divine law. It is not immediately evident, however, just what the character of such a regime would be, for Averroes at no point quits the role of commentator long enough to explain in detail what he envisions. For this reason, but also on the grounds of careful interpretation, it is essential to note that as innovative, iconoclastic, or even unorthodox as this teaching now appears, it cannot reasonably be labeled immoral or unethical. Averroes is intent, above all else, upon organizing the community so that wisdom will rule, for only under such an arrangement do all of the virtues occupy their proper place. This is evident from his account of the reason for the corruption of the various regimes which are inferior to the best regime, from his criticisms of what prevails in his own day, and from the extensive account he gives of the virtues in this work.

Such a line of reasoning inevitably leads back to the third reason given above for Averroes' leaving aside the dialectical arguments of the *Republic,* namely, his desire to set forth his own teaching about the relationship between theory and practice. Though he admits that politics is a practical science (21:8–18), he insists that a city is not well-ordered unless it is ruled by theoretical science (23:18–30, 24:1–6, and 25:5–9). He also argues that in the best city wisdom encompasses more than just the practical arts (48:14–23). For him, the best city can come to be only if the ruler has a grasp of philosophy, and it is the philosopher who is distinguished by his knowledge of the theoretical sciences (60:21–24). It must also be noted that Averroes explicitly calls this point to the attention of his addressee.

Now precisely because Averroes sets this teaching forth by a novel juxtaposition of Plato and Aristotle, it is appropriate to follow out its details as they are elaborated in his *Commentary on Plato's Republic.* There are, to be sure, some subjects which he leaves aside as irrelevant to the major issue. For example, the questions of whether the virtue of liberality should be found in all citizens and whether those citizens beyond the years best suited for siring and bearing children should be permitted to gratify their sexual desires are dismissed with the simple assertion "there is room for inquiry here" (24:10–11 and 56:18–20), which carries the implicit corollary "but not in this work." Other problems apparently seize his interest, but are beyond the scope of this investigation, as, for example, whether certain peoples are more disposed by nature for particular virtues, whether the philosopher-king-imam must also be a prophet—a question to which he promises to return *when* he comments on the *Nicomachean Ethics*—and whether the moral virtues exist for the sake of the practical arts. Averroes singles out such questions by noting "there is room in this for penetrating investigation" (27:7–10, 61:17–18, and 73:1–3). Nonetheless, since he does not investigate those issues here, it seems more appropriate to follow the example he sets with respect to the question of whether the nature of women is the same as the nature of men, one he declares to be "fit for investigation" (53:3–5) and then proceeds to investigate. Taking our questions concerning his precise legislative intentions and how theory can be said to guide practice as equally "fit for investigation," let us now turn to that task. In that enterprise, we shall strive to tell a "fitting story" (31:24–25) about the First Treatise of the commentary, one that is engaging and accurate without being patronizing. Unfortunately, considerations of moderation or, more precisely, proper balance with the other essays in this volume preclude our telling such a "fitting story" about the other two treatises.

**The First Treatise**

The First Treatise is the largest of the three, being more than twice as long as the Second Treatise and longer by half again than the Third Treatise. It may be divided into four major parts: an introduction (21:3–25:9); a long discussion of how to bring about the virtues of courage, moderation, and justice (25:10–52:29); an enumeration of other considerations relevant to the education or formation of the guardians (52:30–60:4); and a conclusion (60:4–16).

The introduction consists of three parts. Averroes begins by declaring his general intention in this work. This statement of purpose is as methodological or procedural as it is substantive; that is, the means and the end are one: He plans to abstract from Plato's *Republic* the scientific statements it contains and thus eliminate the dialectical, all the while speaking as succinctly as he can. He then moves to a general definition of political science, emphasizing that it is a practical rather than a theoretical science, and identifies its particular usefulness as well as its component parts. Averroes proceeds to this introductory account of political science ostensibly because Plato wrote other treatises on politics before composing the *Republic* (21:5–7) and therefore did not bother with such fundamental considerations here. Yet, as has been noted, the framework Averroes then provides is far more representative of Aristotle's teaching than of Plato's and does not even mention any other Platonic works.

Reflection on the subject, principles, and end of politics leads Averroes to classify politics as a practical rather than a theoretical science. As we have already seen, however, he does note that it has something like a theoretical part. This theoretical or general part of politics provides the rules by which subsequent action is to be guided, but does not determine particular courses of action. Even though he does not dwell on the issue here, such distinctions raise the question of what kind of knowledge ultimately guides action. After all, the more general the rules, the closer one comes to theoretical science. Moreover, since it is by means of the art of politics that the city is ordered so as to facilitate each citizen's attaining the perfection for which he or she is suited (23:8–11), the master of the art must be someone who has a clear understanding of human perfection and the way to achieve it, an understanding that can only be theoretical in nature.

Averroes resists this inference and turns instead to the third part of his introduction, an account which explicitly relies on matters discussed in the first part of politics and which explains why man is political by nature. Simply stated, we must live in political communities in order to achieve our personal perfection. Averroes' reasoning is that political association comes about because it is either impossible or extremely unusual for a single man to attain all of the virtues conducive to such perfection. Consequently, men help one another to acquire what makes for good human life. Although such assistance must have originated so that men could more easily acquire the items essential for their survival, Averroes explains how their association contributes to the higher good—the realization of human perfection—before mentioning that it also serves for mere subsistence. He observes further that this natural scarcity of virtue pertains to particular kinds of virtue as well: Wisdom and courage exist only in part of the city, whereas justice and moderation are to be found everywhere (24:7–9).

One reason for Averroes' explaining man's political nature by tracing it to the need human beings have of one another in acquiring the virtues is that he can thereby justify political hierarchy. There would be no reason for political authority, that is, for some people ruling and others being ruled over, if each of the citizens had all of the virtues (see 68:30–69:7). And to the extent that there is a clear hierarchy among the virtues, it is readily evident that those who possess the more lofty virtues should rule over those who do not. At the same time, this argument allows Averroes to show that not all virtue is knowledge and that the virtues are distinct. If all of the citizens can be just and moderate but not wise and courageous, then it is possible to have a certain kind of virtue without having knowledge. Moreover, to the extent that a person can have one or two kinds of virtue without having the others, the virtues are not one.

Despite their being couched in Aristotelian language, these reflections are in keeping with the way the virtues are discussed in the *Republic* (see 432A and 434C). For Socrates, however, the truly virtuous man must have all of the virtues and have them in their fullest condition. Indeed, the goal of the complete education of the guardians is to ensure that they acquire them in just this manner. By allowing that a disjuncture or gap among the virtues may exist even within the confines of this best political community, Socrates does not impugn the validity of the education the guardians receive. To the contrary, this is simply evidence that such an education is not and cannot be extended to all of the citizens. And since no one who does not have all of the virtues can be described as being truly virtuous, the disjuncture is an indication that what usually passes for virtue in political life is not the real thing. The virtues praised in the city, even in this best of all cities—political courage, for example (see *Republic* 430C)—are pale versions of true virtue. This line of reasoning leads to the conclusion that rule by one or a few wise individuals is best because none but the wise can claim to have true virtue.

Averroes hints at such a conclusion (24:1–2), but does not elaborate upon it. Instead he asserts that the account of the virtues of courage, moderation, justice, and wisdom presented in the *Nicomachean Ethics* is adequate and proceeds to outline what must be done here (meaning thereby either Plato's *Republic* or his commentary, the reference being excessively vague) in order to acquire "a complete knowledge of them" (24:13). He identifies three tasks at the outset (24:15–32) and later adds yet another one, almost as an afterthought (25:1–2). To begin with, we need to know what particular conditions must be present in order to bring about the different virtues. Secondly, and here Averroes makes a pointed reference to the parallel between politics and medicine, we need to learn how to establish and develop these virtues in the souls of the youth as well as how to preserve them once they have been acquired and how to eradicate the vices from the souls of the bad. Then, and again Averroes draws explicit attention to the purported parallel with medicine, we must be able to describe which combinations of virtues or habits are conducive to completing these virtues and which are harmful.

Even though Averroes invokes Aristotle's name to insist that the purpose of knowing these things is action, not simply knowledge (24:19–20), there is no escaping the fact that to accomplish these tasks we must have knowledge of the ends of each virtue and of its role in the city. He admits the need for such knowledge, then stresses again the practical ramifications by the afterthought—and in this context he makes it abundantly clear that he is speaking in his own name and of this commentary—that it is also appropriate to explain how each of these virtues comes to be and how they can be brought into existence. The afterthought gives rise to a digression in which Averroes introduces the merit of deliberative virtue and explains, again by reference to medicine, why one who would master politics must have more than knowledge of what this art entails (25:2–9). Nothing in the digression denies the value of knowledge per se. The point is simply that it is not enough only to know; one must be able to do as well. Conversely, it is not possible to do well without knowing what we wish to accomplish: Good political order presupposes precisely this kind of knowledge about the soul and about how the virtues are instilled in it, as well as what purpose they serve. And it is in this sense, if such knowledge is indeed available, that theory can be said to guide practice.

Averroes moves at this point to the second part of the First Treatise, the account of how to bring about the virtues of courage, moderation, and justice. Although he is aware that he should say something about wisdom or intellectual virtue and even promises to do so (39:24–25), he defers that discussion until the Second Treatise. He must do so, for it is there that he discusses the theoretical sciences which provide knowledge of man's end. As Averroes acknowledges here (48:14–29), wisdom can become complete only through the acquisition of such knowledge. In the course of his exposition of the three virtues of courage, moderation, and justice, Averroes devotes the bulk of his discussion to courage and uses it to explain the education of the guardians in gymnastic and music (25:10–49:22), then very cursorily he considers moderation and justice (49:23–52:29). There is a major disproportion between his comments on courage and the education of the guardians in this virtue, on the one hand, and his comments on moderation and justice, on the other, the former being more than seven times longer than the latter. And there is a similar kind of disproportion among the subdivisions of the larger account. Indeed, his discussion of the way the guardians are educated in courage (27:24–42:31) is nearly three times longer than his discussion of the way courage affects the rest of the citizens (43:1–48:29), and the latter is more than six times longer than the account of how courage affects the city as a whole (49:1–22).

Averroes begins with the virtue of courage on the simple grounds that it is the virtue with which Plato began (25:10–11). By the end of the discussion, however, it is patent that Averroes had to begin with courage. It seems to be the master virtue. After all, the guardians acquire moderation and justice as a result of their education in courage (39:24–42:31). Clearly, there is something circumstantial about such an argument: Courage has such broad influence here because Averroes is describing the part of the city in which it is most properly found. Yet the argument goes further, insofar as courage is the fundamental characteristic of the guardians and they are the mainstay of the city (50:4–5 and 49:16–22). Moreover, courage is said to have a preservative force: Without it, people would readily surrender their opinions—especially the beneficial ones—and the whole education they have undergone would then be to no avail (39:6–23 and 52:5–7).

Still, there is something unsatisfactory about calling courage the master virtue. After all, by presenting it first, Averroes has no occasion to explain how it relates to wisdom. Only if the guardian's education in music could be said to take the place of wisdom would this interpretation be sound. Yet this education is explicitly identified as being conducted by means of similes and imitations (29:13–30:13). Not even the fact that those responsible for designing the guardians' education in music do have theoretical knowledge (48:19–21) is sufficient to overcome the objection. Moreover, by intimating that justice is secured by education in courage, Averroes goes against this later claim that justice guarantees the acquisition not only of moderation and courage, but also of wisdom (see 50:14–15 with 49:24–50:10). Elsewhere as well, Averroes states the overwhelming importance of justice in utterly unequivocal, albeit dialectical, terms by noting that there would be no need for courage if all of the citizens were just, whereas there is always a need for justice even if they are all courageous.[16] Finally, this explanation of

[16] See *Talkhīṣ Kitāb al-Jadal,* par. 109.

courage goes against the earlier statement that justice and moderation are more widespread, for it surely means that they exist independently of courage (see above, p. 30 and references).

By drawing attention to courage in this manner, Averroes forces the reader to think again about the way he presents this virtue. Such reflection leads to the observation that the elaborate three- or four-point outline of what yet needs to be done in order to obtain complete knowledge of the virtues does not in fact guide the subsequent discussion and that the substantive account of courage brings Averroes into explicit disagreement with Plato on two points. After declaring his intention to investigate courage, Averroes reminds the reader of his earlier summary of the three-point outline, namely, that to understand how to bring the virtues about it is necessary to know what is intended by the action of each of them in the city (see 25:11–13 with 24:30–32). But he drops the subject immediately and concentrates instead on an explanation of the two general ways by which the virtues are brought about, persuasion and coercion. Both of these ways are said to be natural (25:32–33 and 26:7–10), an attribute he does not ascribe to the "true ways"—that is, the education in logic, mathematics, optics, mechanics, physics, and First Philosophy or metaphysics—by which the few guardian chiefs learn the theoretical sciences (see 25:15–18 with 74:14–78:9). Although coercion has its place, Averroes prefers to use persuasion to educate the guardians. And he presents their education in such a manner as to fulfill indirectly two of the tasks called for in the earlier outline: His account of the basic nature of the guardians (27:24–29:9) corresponds to the first point, stating the conditions for the realization of the virtues, whereas the whole discussion of the education in gymnastic and music (29:9–39:5) corresponds to the second, explaining how they may be established.

That Averroes thinks it possible to instill virtue in the citizens by means of persuasion, that is, by recourse to rhetoric and poetics, is readily understandable. As he notes, it is not to be expected that the many will come to know the theoretical sciences by means of demonstrative arguments, such reasoning being beyond the grasp of most people (25:19–33). Now this implies that insofar as Averroes really considers his commentary to contain only scientific or demonstrative arguments abstracted from Plato's *Republic,* he intends it for a limited audience. The many can be induced to believe things pertaining to the theoretical sciences by means of persuasion. Such belief helps them do what they ought to do and would quite probably not do otherwise; it encourages them to do certain kinds of good deeds habitually. Yet this kind of inducing can be justified only if the actions it encourages are truly virtuous. There are two ways of knowing that they are so. One is to know about the whole, that is, as Socrates would say, to have an idea of the good. The other is to observe how these actions function in everyday political life and to reflect upon the things people praise or strive for, somewhat in the manner of Aristotle. Here, Averroes seems to follow the lead of Socrates (29:37–30:13).

Before reaching the issue of how recourse to persuasion can be justified, however, it is appropriate to consider what Averroes has to say about the other means of instilling virtue in the souls of the citizens, coercion. If coercion, which is a form of warfare, is used with respect to another nation or group of people so as to instruct them in what is ultimately for their own good, then such coercion or warfare appears to be just. The basic condition for using it, then, is that those against whom it is employed can learn to be virtuous. Courage is the virtue which guides those who use coercion: It gives them the strength to persevere in what is otherwise a most unpleasant undertaking and keeps them ever mindful of their educative goal. At the same time, coercion or warfare is the natural end of courage: The role of courage in the city is to prepare it for warlike enterprises designed to discipline or educate other cities with which it must deal (26:14–26). The political community that uses courage to such ends does not exploit other political communities. Although it is confident about its understanding of virtue, so confident as to force recalcitrant peoples to adopt its own ways, it sees no reason to profit from the pursuit of courage.

Noting here that Aristotle and Farabi agree on this point, Averroes sides with them against what he alleges to be Plato's opinion, namely, that courage is for the sake of warfare against other nations, either to plunder their wealth or to ensure the security of the fatherland from both actual and anticipated attacks (26:26–32). In attributing this opinion to Plato, Averroes seems to be thinking of the discussion in Book Four of the *Republic* in which Socrates explains to Adeimantus that the virtuous city will be able to defend itself against far more powerful nations by aligning itself with other nations through a promise to give them the wealth of the defeated powerful nations, wealth for which the austerely raised guardians of the virtuous city have no use (422A–E). In reality, then, both arguments come to the same conclusion: Courage entails aggression against those who either do or might threaten the well-being of one's own city. Averroes objects to this understanding of courage because he considers it to presuppose too much of one's own fellow citizens. It could be justified only on the grounds that "there were but one class of humans disposed to the human perfections and especially to the theoretical ones." Plato's error, he contends, is to view the Greeks in such a light (27:1–3).

Insisting that only the educative function of coercion excuses its use, Averroes goes a step further and limits justifiable coercion to the young. His argument is that it is usually not possible to reform adults who have been brought up badly. Consequently, only the extent of coercion needed to take their children from such adults and then raise them in virtue is warranted (27:14–18). This suggestion foreshadows Averroes' subsequent endorsement of Socrates' outrageous proposal to Glaucon at the end of Book VII that all citizens over the age of ten will be expelled from the city and their children raised according to the education already set forth (see 78:16–26 with *Republic* 540E–541B).

Averroes' disagreement with Plato here, like his later disagreement concerning the size and number of virtuous communities (46:15–25), takes place in the shadow of the revealed law of Islam. A number of Quranic passages urge believers to struggle in the way of God, both in the sense of struggling against one's desires and in the sense of struggling against those who oppose the true faith of Islam. Of the latter passages, a few verses insist that struggling against or fighting with disbelievers may lead them to change their beliefs and practices. Coercion, then, can be used effectively against those brought up wrongly, whatever their age (see Quran, ii.190–193 and ix.29).[17] Given his praise of Islamic revealed law earlier in his discussion of courage for its conformity to human law (26:16–18)—the word "law" in both instances being rendered by the Hebrew *torah,* itself undoubtedly a translation of the Arabic *sharīʿah*—it is not surprising that Averroes would make such a criticism. If anything, it is even less surprising when we recall that this work is addressed to a highly restricted audience.

Before considering Averroes' other explicit disagreement with Plato, it seems appropriate to say something about how the guardians are in fact educated in courage. The principle guiding their education is related to the opinion that justice consists in each person's doing his own particular work and dictates that no one should acquire more than one art (see 27:24–28:6 with 23:31–33). Gymnastic and music are the means by which they are to be educated, gymnastic so that they might acquire true bodily virtue and music so that the soul might be disciplined and thereby acquire virtue (29:9–12). The education in music precedes that in gymnastic because the mind seems to be ready for instruction before the body is for exercise. However that may be, the education in music is presented solely in negative terms and consists of a series of explanations about the restrictions to be placed on stories or fables, imitations, melodies, and rhythms (30:14–36:23). Following Socrates, Averroes emphasizes the importance of protecting the young guardians from false and base stories; stories which give rise to the fear of death; and stories which prompt laughter, further falsehood, or incite to

[17]See also 60:1–4 and Lerner's note containing Averroes' remarks in his *Middle Commentary on Aristotle's Nicomachean Ethics* about the erroneous way in which Muslims usually interpret these injunctions. For the Latin text of this passage, see *In libros decem Moralium Nicomachiorum,* fol. 79F–G. See also Rosenthal, *Averroes' Commentary on Plato's Republic,* pp. 258–259, and *Jihad in Mediaeval and Modern Islam,* trans. Rudolph Peters (Leiden: E. J. Brill, 1977), pp. 11–19 and 23–25.

pleasure. Clearly, along with fortifying them to hardship, such an austere education makes them almost insensitive to pleasure.

Yet while forbidding false stories along with those which further falsehood, Averroes, like Socrates, insists that it is permissible, even beneficial, for the rulers to lie to the citizen (32:17–22), and approvingly cites a story he considers to have been cleverly, or perhaps prudently, set forth in the *Republic* (40:6–41:4). The story, which Socrates calls a noble or well-born lie (*pseudos gennaion*) and thinks of as being opportune or timely (*en deonti*), is meant to persuade the citizens to accept the rigid class stratification of the virtuous city (see *Republic* III, 414C–415C). Nor is it the only clever lie used with them, the only way in which they are tricked. When discussing the arrangements for procreation among the guardians in the third part of this treatise, Averroes dwells at length on the care which must be taken to ensure that the good natures of the parents are passed on to the offspring. For those guardians of the appropriate age to sire and bear children, extremely elaborate wedding ceremonies are organized. Because all of the guardians are equal in principle, there is no reason for any to have marked preferences for others, especially since the weddings last only until the women become pregnant. Consequently, equity requires that the guardians be paired off by a completely nonarbitrary system, for example, the drawing of lots. Once such an arrangement is instituted, the particular marriage couples become simply the result of chance. Yet since the outcome of such a lottery is so important to the well-being of the city, the rulers tamper with the lots so that "the good kind of women are allotted to the good kind of men, and the bad to the bad, without any of the citizens other than the lords being aware of this" (55:1–23; see also 56:22–24). By dubbing the first lie—which is not all that different in purpose from the second—as "well-born," Socrates seems to have hit upon a characterization which is equally suitable for the latter.

Whatever else might be said against such clever lies, it is clear that they deprive the guardians of free choice. Yet if their education does not contribute to their wise use of freedom, how can it truly be called an education in virtue? Virtuous conduct, as we know from the first part of this art, requires informed and free choice (see *Nicomachean Ethics* III.v.1113$^{b}$3–13 and 1114$^{b}$17–25). The only members of the city who seem to have such freedom are the rulers, the very ones who tell the lies and manipulate the lots. They—and it must never be forgotten that their counterparts in the cities of our acquaintance are lawgivers and founders—make the arbitrary seem necessary and the naturally attractive repulsive. They do so to help those for whom they legislate attain true happiness. Nonetheless, insofar as they use lies, untrue stories, and acts of deception so that the citizens will follow their prescriptions, they keep them from acquiring true virtue. Averroes seems to acknowledge as much by the way he distinguishes between the true virtue the guardians acquire through gymnastic, on the one hand, and the discipline of the soul plus limited virtue they acquire through music, on the other (see 29:9–12 with 36:6–23). Although he does not claim that either gymnastic or music leads to unqualifiedly true virtue, he does emphasize that gymnastic, which makes no use of deception, leads to a more genuine kind of virtue than music.

Troubling as these reflections are, they do not invalidate the goals of this or any other city whose lawgiver deceives the citizens so that they will do what is for their ultimate benefit and would otherwise not do. Precisely because not all human beings are capable of perfect virtue, recourse must be had to such devices to bring those less qualified to the similitudes within their reach. The sacrifices demanded of the guardians are, as Averroes observes, mere trifles when compared to the sound discipline they receive (46:22–31). That he does characterize them as trifles given the larger goal they secure takes on greater significance when it is noted that just before doing so he speaks of this city as the one "that we are involved in bringing forth" (45:13; see also 44:28–29), rather than just "this city which we are describing in speech" (26:11–12) or "this city that we have described in speech" (64:27). Moreover, he characterizes the sacrifices as trifles in the course of marking his second explicit disagreement with Plato, a disagreement which has its roots in his own interpretation of one of the Prophet Muhammad's sayings and then leads to an extensive discussion of the way the different kinds of laws ought to function.

There is a common thread between this disagreement and the earlier one, Averroes' dismay that Plato singles out the Greeks and pays no heed to other peoples. Averroes finds that predilection coming to the fore again insofar as Plato provides for only one virtuous city in the *Republic* and is content that it be quite limited in size. For Averroes, however, several such cities are needed which, whatever their size, must eventually embrace the surface of the temperate zones (46:17–18; see also 27:11–13). He has recourse to the authority of the Prophet and cites his statement "I have been sent to the Red and the Black" to buttress his own position. Then, should such an appeal to authority not be sufficient, Averroes indicates that Aristotle is also of the same opinion and asserts that "it is the indubitable truth."

The passage is remarkable for three reasons. First, to the best of my recollection, nowhere else in this treatise does Averroes call upon the Prophet Muhammad as an authority. To the contrary, much of what is set forth here is in tension with the legislation set forth by Muhammad. Secondly, an appeal to authority—whether it be to the Prophet Muhammad or to Aristotle—is more suitable for dialectical or rhetorical than for demonstrative argumentation. In the latter, only sound syllogisms are acceptable. Finally, as in the previous disagreement, Averroes rejects an opinion of Plato's and adopts in its stead one of Aristotle's. It seems as though Plato's excesses must be tempered by Aristotle, as though Aristotle has the last word both with respect to the second part of politics and with respect to the first.

Then, after dismissing the hardships imposed on the guardians as trifles, Averroes explains how the general laws (*toroth,* i.e., *sharāʾiʿ*) and the general nomoi strive towards the same goals. In the course of this explanation (46:27–47:28), it becomes clear that the laws laid down for this city are nomoi—general nomoi. Throughout the whole work, Averroes defends the soundness of these nomoi. He notes that other general laws sometimes accomplish the same ends as the general nomoi and that divine laws have a more restricted sphere. Although he earlier calls upon Muhammad's authority to refute Plato, he is now content to follow Plato's lead and to restrict the divine law to regulating how God and the angels might best be praised as well as to ensuring observance of the other kinds of divine commands revealed through prophecy. The concerns of the divine law seem, then, to be partial, while those of the general laws and the general nomoi are much broader. The spheres of influence are so drawn that the divine law does not replace or invalidate the general laws and general nomoi, nor do they replace or invalidate it. Rather, the divine law complements, perhaps even completes, them.

The discussion leads to reflections on the place of wisdom in the city (48:14–29), which are occasioned by Averroes' account of how the conversation in the *Republic* was transformed from an original desire to investigate justice in the individual soul to an investigation of the way it functions in a larger entity like a city. Brief as they are, the reflections are considered by Averroes to provide a sufficient account of the role of wisdom in the city: A summary statement immediately follows this interlude, and Averroes then observes that "it remains for us to speak of the two remaining virtues, namely moderation and justice" (49:23). His account of wisdom centers around the idea that it embodies the understanding of the ends to which all of the laws and nomoi are directed. Even though such wisdom becomes manifest as "good governance and good counsel," it is not to be confused with skill, knowledge, or wisdom in the practical arts. He insists instead that the wisdom needed for the city is that stemming from knowledge of man's end, knowledge acquired through the pursuit of the theoretical sciences. Such knowledge is the preserve of the philosophers, and they rule the city according to what they know about what human beings ought to do.

The deceit practiced upon the guardians who eventually become rulers is justified, then, because it makes them accept a discipline necessarily preliminary to the pursuit of the theoretical sciences. Before human beings can engage in such study, they must have a certain kind of moral character. Only after the habits corresponding to that character are firmly rooted in the individual soul can the deeper questioning which leads to intellectual and moral virtue be allowed. In the Second Treatise, the discussion focuses on why such a moral character is requisite and on the end for the sake of which such deceptive means are employed.

Now, however, the question as to what justifies deception with respect to the ordinary guardians, the ones who will not become rulers, has yet to be resolved. As is somehow fitting, the elements of an answer are contained in Averroes' final account of justice (50:10–52:29), an account which follows what can only be described as a very moderate explanation of moderation (49:24–50:10). When speaking of the wisdom which consists of understanding the ends aimed at by the laws and the nomoi as well as the end of human existence, Averroes emphasized the role of the theoretical sciences. Similarly, when he first explained the parallels between the human virtues and the parts of the city, he distinguished between the rational or theoretical part, the spirited part, and the appetitive part (23:18–30, esp. 23:18–22). In the present context, he speaks in a more restricted manner. He identifies the rational or theoretical part as calculating (51:9–11) and makes wisdom consist in cogitative or deliberative excellence (52:8–9; see also 52:4). The tension between the various parts of the soul is quite prevalent in this discussion, and the need for the spirited and appetitive parts to be dominated is constantly stressed. They can be brought under control as long as the basic notion of justice as each individual performing his own tasks—or each part its own function—is rigidly observed (51:11–52:3). I take it that the same understanding of the need to dominate the nonrational elements excuses the recourse to deception with respect to the guardians who will not become philosophers and with respect to the other members of the city. Not all citizens can aspire to the kind of freedom essential for the virtue and eventual happiness of the philosopher-rulers. There is something like a natural scarcity of human virtue. Just as it renders human beings political by nature, it also introduces a fundamental inequality among them. Still, the less gifted can aspire to a different kind of happiness, one more suited to their talents. Its attainment requires them to observe the rule of justice which guides this city, but its worth is not diminished by their being tricked or even coerced into observing it. A lesser happiness than that of the philosopher-ruler, it is by no means a false or errant happiness.

This completes the discussion about the way the virtues are brought about, and Averroes now turns "to what remains in the case of the guardians, namely the inquiry concerning how they copulate, the upbringing of their children, and the manner of their procreation" (52:28–29). Though he claims to be following Plato's return to this subject, his remarks about the relationship between women's natures and men's are without parallel in Plato's text (52:30–54:16). To underline that he is speaking in his own name, Averroes frequently employs the first person plural and points to the evils existing in the cities of his day because of the way women's capacities are understood.

Even when he does rejoin the text of the *Republic,* he continues to speak frequently in his own name (see 54:17–21, 54:27–55:27, 56:22–57:4, and 57:23–25). In addition to the arranged marriages, which have already been discussed, Averroes accepts the idea that equality between men and women requires the women to join the men in exercising without clothing and the notion that children should be held in common. In fact, he considers the community of women and children to be "one of the most necessary of things" for the unity of the city (57:23–25; see also 57:26–58:18).

Then Averroes turns to a series of considerations respecting warfare and embraces the suggestions that the children of the city attend battles as spectators from a very early age, that good warriors receive special distinctions and the highest of honors, and that fellow citizens who revolt not be reduced to slavery (58:15–60:4). The recommendation that the children watch battles prompts Averroes to become one of the rulers momentarily. Keeping alive the recourse to deception so widely used in the education of the guardians, he notes, speaking in his own name, that "we shall *cunningly* provide for their security" by giving them steady, old horses to ride and by placing them in a safe place from which they may view the battle (59:3; emphasis added). The children thus experience warfare and are allowed to believe that they are being exposed to its dangers so that they might become inured to them, without the city at any time really risking the lives of its future guardians. They are tricked into becoming accustomed to warfare, just as their parents were tricked into the activities leading to their birth. Averroes' remarks about not enslaving fellow citizens who revolt prompt him to urge that the rebels be viewed as errant citizens and treated accordingly, not as people who have rejected the traditions of the city, that is, as unbelievers. While endorsing this argument of the *Republic* and recasting it so that it applies to a concern central to Islamic statecraft, he is content to state simply that "what Plato asserts differs from what many Lawgivers assert" (60:4). Nonetheless, like his earlier attempt to limit the use of coercion, this statement shows that Averroes is quite willing to distance himself from the traditional views of his own community (see above, note 17 and context).

All of the explanations about the additional regulations concerning the education of the guardians are presented in positive terms. They all center upon the life of the community. As proof that they are beneficial, Averroes frequently contrasts them and the way their implementation would affect the city with the ill-conceived practices of his own day. Now it is possible to read the proposals regarding the community of women and children as instances of Socratic irony which suggest that even this best of all cities makes such outrageous demands upon its citizens as to render its own existence ultimately undesirable, even if it could come into being.[18] Averroes, however,

[18] See Allan Bloom's interpretive essay accompanying his translation, *The Republic of Plato* (New York: Basic Books, 1968), pp. 380–388 and 409–412; and Leo Strauss, *The City and Man* (Chicago: Rand McNally and Company, 1964), pp. 114–119 and 121–128.

does nothing of the kind. He embraces these and similar suggestions as both desirable and necessary.

In the conclusion, Averroes observes that he has now explained what Plato says about the education of the guardians and how it brings about community among them. He also draws attention to the general applicability of the education for the other classes within the city. Finally, he acknowledges the necessity of speaking about "the class of the wise" and offers a three-point outline of how that subject will be treated in the following treatise, an outline to which he does adhere. His desire to speak about the "class of the wise" is prompted by the discussion of how such rulers are to be educated, a discussion which begins near the end of Book Five of the *Republic* (472A) when Socrates introduces the "third wave," that is, the need for philosophers to rule or for those who rule to pursue philosophy, and continues through Book Seven (541B).

As was mentioned above, considerations of space preclude following out both Averroes' discussion of the education of the wise and the topics expounded in the Third Treatise. It does seem appropriate, however, to restate the major themes of the preceding exposition and their implications. First, though commenting on Plato's *Republic,* Averroes couches his remarks in a peculiarly Aristotelian manner even when doing so obliges him to stretch the meaning of Plato's arguments. Moreover, on the two occasions when he finds it necessary to differ with Plato, he asserts his agreement with Aristotle. It seems as though Averroes recognizes the merit of Plato's teaching as long as it is in accord with Aristotle's and opts for Aristotle's when there is discord between the two. Nonetheless, many of his suggestions about the relationship between theory and practice show that he shares Plato's opinion about the need for, and the possibility of, theory guiding practice. His endorsement of this opinion means that he must modify his account of the scarcity of the virtues: Though certain individuals or classes of individuals may have only one or two virtues, those who direct the city according to wisdom must have all of the virtues. The basic premise in all of this, a premise patently at odds with Aristotle's teaching, is that it is possible to use demonstrative reasoning with respect to practical matters.

Secondly, Averroes reads the *Republic* as though the discussion concerning the virtuous city were aimed at bringing this city into being and he speaks as though his comments here were directed towards the same goal. For example, he frequently reflects on how the different institutions and educational practices influence human character and endorses them because of the advantages they embody. On such occasions he inevitably contrasts them with the practices prevalent in the cities of his own day and always finds those practices worthy of blame. And he does so even when he is thereby obliged to embrace patently outrageous suggestions or to put himself at odds with traditions understood by his contemporaries as deriving from a divine source.

One consequence is that when Averroes does speak about the divine law, he presents it as being judged by its conformity to human law and as more restricted in scope than either general human laws or the general nomoi. Correct as he may be on the former point, insofar as we have no other rational criteria by which to judge the divine law and must therefore use our own natural lights, his latter position is more difficult to maintain. If nothing else, it simply must be acknowledged that no divine law—and certainly not the one of his own community—views itself as partial or as restricted in scope.

Finally, Averroes' discussion of courage and the guardians' education in courage points to the question of the hierarchy among the virtues. By dint of their training in courage, the guardians come to have moderation and justice. However, the way this training is carried out deprives them of the full acquisition of either virtue. At most, they learn self-restraint and tending to their own business. The fuller education in each of these virtues is reserved for a select group of the guardians, those who will eventually become rulers. They go beyond the limitations of this first education because they investigate for themselves the ends for the sake of which it is ordered. Despite the limitations of this first education, however, virtue still remains more important than ethics. The training, discipline, or habituation in courage as well as in moderation and justice which characterizes this First Treatise is in the service of a higher goal. It is, then, a means rather than an end.

## Conclusion

The argument of the Second Treatise shows that some of these conclusions are premature. For example, it becomes apparent in the Second Treatise that our understanding of the master virtue must be revised. The enumeration of the virtues central to the major argument of Plato's *Republic* and to that of the First Treatise—wisdom, courage, moderation, and justice—is modified substantially in the course of the Second Treatise. The single most important change is a new enumeration which, while taking these four virtues into account, assigns them a different rank and introduces yet other virtues. Whereas Socrates never adequately explains whether he means by wisdom theoretical or practical knowledge and Averroes is equally vague in the First Treatise, in the Second he clearly distinguishes between the two. Theoretical virtue or science is the highest human perfection. Immediately subordinate to it is the most comprehensive deliberative virtue, the one crucial for the art of ruling cities: prudence or practical wisdom. Though theoretical virtue does not minister to deliberative virtue, the philosopher-ruler draws the basic principles of sound rule from his attainment of the former. In this sense, then, theoretical virtue comes forth as the master virtue in the Second Treatise. Moreover, deliberative virtue or prudence is presented as being higher in rank than any of the moral virtues. Since justice, moderation, and courage are classified as moral virtues in the Second Treatise, deliberative virtue is higher in rank than any of them. And as the ranking now stands, courage is so far from being the master virtue that it is actually presented as being subordinate to moderation.

It has already been pointed out that the major part of Averroes' discussion in the Second Treatise relies on Aristotelian doctrines rather than on Socratic or Platonic ones. Yet at no point does he consider it necessary to draw explicit attention to this fact or to suggest that the revisions of his earlier arguments be understood in the light of such a change. The early training of the guardians can proceed according to the terms set out in roughly the first half of the *Republic,* but their more specialized education must draw its principles from other sources. A change is needed so that the hierarchy among the virtues will become evident and their link to political life affirmed. Under optimal conditions, the pursuit of the ultimate human good cannot be in conflict with the demands of the city (see 78:7–9).

In other words, the simply best regime is one in which the natural order among the virtues and practical arts is respected. The practical arts and the moral virtues exist for the sake of the deliberative virtues, and—whatever the hierarchical relationship between the practical arts and the moral virtues—all of these exist for the sake of the theoretical virtues. Only when this natural order is reflected in the organization and administration of the regime can there be any assurance that all of the virtues and practical arts will function as they ought. In order to have sound practice, then, it is necessary to understand the principles on which such practice depends: the order and the interrelationship among the parts of the human soul.

That moral virtue exists for the sake of theoretical virtue means that it may be acquired prior to theoretical virtue. We first come to have moral virtue on the basis of unexamined opinion. Then, as we practice it and become more schooled in the various sciences, we may eventually acquire deliberative and even theoretical virtue. Once we do acquire the latter, we discern the principles of true moral virtue and are then able to revise our earlier understanding which was based on unexamined opinion.

Having once discerned these principles, Averroes can also judge the shortcomings in the regimes he sees around him more clearly. These regimes are to be faulted either because they aim at the wrong kind of end or because they fail to respect any order among the human virtues. It is in his criticism of the regimes of his day that Averroes shows himself most clearly as a lawgiver. His blame of democracy for the emphasis it places on the private and for its inability to order the desires of the citizens is complemented by his earlier presentation of what distinguishes the virtuous regime. Thus in the

First Treatise he shows how to foster greater concern for the public sphere and diminish the appeal of the private. Similarly, his exposition of man's ultimate happiness in the Second Treatise indicates how the desires should be properly ordered.

There are nonetheless some aspects of this positive teaching which give us pause. However persuasive Averroes' arguments about the goodness of the best regime and the evils of the alternatives to it, we cannot fail to notice that the means he advocates for bringing this regime about and preserving it once it has come into existence are immoral and unethical. Without hesitation, he advocates a lie to justify the class stratification fundamental to it. He also endorses deceptions concerning the equitable distribution of marriage partners, the way children will be accustomed to warfare, and the education of the wise. In addition, he approves of the proposition that older citizens who have allowed this regime to come into being will be expelled from it just as it is about to take shape. Averroes accepts these lies, deceptions, and injustices because he contends that the plain truth is not always persuasive, that reason does not usually prevail. Most adults are like children in that they need to be trained to do what is right, and such training requires compulsion as well as deception. Unless the citizens can be induced to believe in a good that transcends their own immediate well-being, they will not make the sacrifices frequently necessary for the establishment and functioning of the virtuous regime. Though a few may eventually come to understand why they must place the public good before their own private well-being and why they must subordinate their immediate desires to a more distant good, most will not. Moreover, to assure the improvement of many, it may be necessary to abandon others to their own devices. Because the end he seeks is itself good, Averroes is content to pursue it by such deceptive, even immoral, means. In this sense, the pursuit of virtue sometimes requires one to perform unethical actions.

Averroes' perception of the hierarchy among the virtues, especially the political implications of that hierarchy, and his conviction that man can attain his ultimate perfection only within a political community justify in Averroes' eyes such infringements of moral principles. However it comes about and whatever means it uses to prolong its life, the best city is absolutely necessary if human beings are to attain their ultimate human perfection. Precisely this line of reasoning dictates the subordination of particular revealed laws to the human laws and the praise of this best city even though it is ordered only according to general nomoi: The general nomoi are derived from reflection about human perfection and are guided by the strictures of human law as understood in philosophy.

It must be noticed, however, that Averroes also resorts to less explicit hints of deception. Among these are his pairing of the *Republic* with the *Politics* in order to juxtapose them to the *Nicomachean Ethics,* his substitution of passages from several other Aristotelian treatises for Books One and

Two and Books Six and Seven of the *Republic,* respectively, and his substitution of logic for mathematics as well as several other disciplines for dialectic in the curriculum by which the wise are to be educated. In addition, he indirectly criticizes Islamic precepts, uses dialectical and rhetorical arguments despite his many claims that this commentary is concerned only with theoretical arguments, and alters Plato's list of the different kinds of regimes. However reasonable Averroes' endorsement of recourse to explicit lies and acts of injustice, given the need to establish the virtuous regime and the acknowledged limitations of most human beings, his use of these more concealed instances of deception is not so readily understandable. Not least among the objections to them is that they are meant to deceive us, the readers of this commentary.

One consequence of Averroes' many manipulations of Plato's text is to make that teaching appear more Aristotelian in tone. At the same time, these manipulations portray Aristotle's teaching as being in closer harmony with Plato's. Averroes does not seek to reject Plato for Aristotle, nor Aristotle for Plato, but to present them both as making eminently reasonable and quite similar arguments. When the two come into irreconcilable conflict, he favors Aristotle. Aristotle's practical inclination or willingness to respect the limits of this world provides a needed correction to Plato's more fanciful suggestions and conviction that the life devoted to wisdom is incompatible with the life of political action. Conversely, Averroes interprets Aristotle's account of the intellectual virtues in the light of Plato's insistence that wisdom or theoretical knowledge must guide practice. In sum, then, Averroes' novel interpretation of these two authorities leads to his own political teaching becoming more readily acceptable.

Related to this is the simple fact that Averroes has not demonstrated anything about man's ultimate perfection. We do not really know now what virtue or the good is, even though we have a clearer idea of what it might resemble and are much more aware of how we should investigate it further. By revealing what Averroes has so artfully concealed, I by no means wish to imply that it is impossible to arrive at a clear apprehension of either virtue or the good. My point is, rather, that such an investigation is long and arduous. It does need to be undertaken by the study of other subjects and thus cannot possibly be summarized in a few lines. Consequently, Averroes tells as likely or as fitting a story about it as he can and remains silent about its problematic aspects. To show us how to examine opposing arguments based on generally accepted opinions, the evils to which our pursuit of the wrong goals can lead, and even how to direct our inquiry into the ultimate human perfection is not sufficient; he must also ensure the possibility of further investigation. Paradoxical though it may seem, the best way for him to accomplish that task is to present his teaching in such an obscure and sometimes misleading fashion.

# ETHICS IN ISLAMIC TRADITIONALIST DOCTRINE

GEORGE MAKDISI
University of Pennsylvania

Ethics is a science that seeks to know which actions should be done and which avoided. It is a practical science; it seeks knowledge not for the sake of knowledge, it seeks it in order to apply it. This quest is what most typified the Traditionalists in Islam. It set them apart from the Rationalists. They believed the Rationalists to be less mindful of actions, more occupied with words, "kalām." They believed them to be too involved with philosophical speculation, too engrossed in matters beyond man's capacity to know, too taken up with questions about God Himself. For the Traditionalists, this is not the proper business of Islam. Whereas the Rationalists concentrated on philosophical theology, kalām, the Traditionalists concerned themselves with law; and law and legal theory, being normative, were closer to ethics.

The central concern of Islam is man's actions: his obligations to God's word as expressed in His commands and prohibitions. It is a system of moral obligations. It shies away from speculation about God, considering it man's fruitless attempt to acquire a knowledge that could never be adequate to its object. Such is the concern of Traditionalism. From Islam's early centuries down to our times this concern has been given expression by the adherents of Traditionalism. The following passage was written by a twelfth-century Traditionalist in refutation of a member of his own school, a fellow Traditionalist who had strayed off the beaten path of Traditionalist thought and into that of theological speculation:

> We have no need to know the meaning which God intended by His attributes; no course of *action* is intended by them, nor is there any *obligation* attached to them, except to believe them, and it is possible to believe them without the *knowledge* of their intended sense. For indeed faith, with ignorance, is sound.[1]

[1] Ibn Qudāma (d. 620/1223), *Taḥrīm an-naẓar fī kūtub ahl al-kalām,* in G. Makdisi, *Ibn Qudāma's Censure of Speculative Theology,* Arabic text edited with English translation and introduction, E. J. W. Gibb Memorial, n.s. 23 (London: Luzac, 1962), p. 22/32, §55. This work was written in refutation of a fellow Hanbali, Ibn ʿAqīl (d. 513/1119).

No *action* is intended by them; no *obligation* is attached to them; *faith, without knowledge, is sound.* God obligates us to certain acts of commission and omission; He demands of us faith in the Scriptures. Such are the chief components of the Traditionalist Creed. Knowledge based on speculation is not a necessary component.

This position is not peculiar to the author of this passage, nor is it peculiar to a handful of thinkers like him, or even to his own period. The author was giving expression to a mental attitude already a commonplace in Traditionalist thought. It does not merely go as far back as the third/ninth-century Ibn Ḥanbal, eponym of the school to which the author belongs. It goes further back to the first champion of Traditionalism, to Shāfiᶜī, eponym of another school of law, who was the first successfully to challenge Rationalism toward the end of the second century of the hijra. The message of Shāfiᶜī is not different, in its essence, from that of Ibn Qudāma of the twelfth century, or even from that of Ibn Taimīya of the fourteenth, whose works have had a profound influence on Traditionalist movements down to our times. There is a distance of five centuries separating Shāfiᶜī and Ibn Taimīya. In that span of time the attitude of Traditionalism toward Rationalism remained essentially the same: antagonistic. But Traditionalism, especially as represented by thinkers like Ibn Taimīya, had become more sophisticated, had learned to use the weapons of Rationalism, and had, above all, learned to discriminate between men and ideas. A predecessor of Ibn Taimīya, a fellow-Hanbali of the eleventh-twelfth century, believed that one should be ready to accept the truth wherever one happened to find it: A jewel in a dunghill is no less a jewel for being there.[2]

Traditionalist thought did not stand still during the five centuries between Shāfiᶜī and Ibn Taimīya. On the contrary, it developed and evolved to such an extent that the first fathers of the movement would have had trouble recognizing some of the positions taken by their spiritual heirs. Ibn ᶜAqīl was accused of Muᶜtazilism, not without some justice, but nevertheless remained a Hanbali and lived a half-century thereafter to influence a long line of followers; and Ibn Taimīya, popularly considered as a die-hard Traditionalist of ultraconservative tendencies, even accused of the crassest anthropomorphism, gave expression to teachings which, coming from a Traditionalist, are startling, to say the least. His concept of secondary causes is nothing short of astonishing in an Islam generally considered to be dominated by a philosophy of occasionalism.

Yet there is a direct connection between Ibn Taimīya and the first great champion of Traditionalism, Shāfiᶜī. Certain key statements of Shāfiᶜī, in

[2] Ibn ᶜAqīl, as quoted in later works; see G. Makdisi, *The Rise of Colleges: Institutions of Learning in Islam and the West* (Edinburgh: The University Press, 1981), p. 258 and n. 159 on p. 340.

the introduction to his work known as the *Risāla,*[3] are the very basis of Ibn Taimīya's treatise entitled *Maᶜārij al-wuṣūl.*[4] Both authors say, in effect, that all that is needed for salvation is contained in the Holy Scriptures. In other words, there is no real need to go any further than the Koran and the sunna.

This thesis is at the very basis of Shāfiᶜī's *Risāla,* the treatise that was acclaimed as the first comprehensive work on the fundamentals of the revealed law (*uṣūl al-fiqh*). In my opinion, the *Risāla* is Shāfiᶜī's answer to the speculations of the Muᶜtazila about God. Shāfiᶜī meant his *Risāla* to be the antidote to Muᶜtazili kalām.[5] To this kalām, this philosophical theology of the Muᶜtazila, Shāfiᶜī wished to oppose an elaborate science of comparable scope, not merely to cope with the growing influence of Rationalist thought in Muslim intellectual circles, but to deflect the course of kalām away from the mainstream of Islamic thought. Muᶜtazilism remained as a tributary, even a very strong tributary, but because of the efforts of Shāfiᶜī and his successors, the bulk of the waters carried by Islam's mainstream flowed in from unmistakably Traditionalist sources. Shāfiᶜī's message was that the business of Islam is to concentrate on God's commands and prohibitions, for that is the way to know what is good in order to do it, and what is evil in order to avoid it. This meant that Islam's business is not to concentrate on God Himself, not to pit one's mind against the Almighty, a dangerous business because fraught with the danger of heresy, with the danger of rivaling with one's own Maker, and a useless business to boot, at best leading nowhere; at worst, leading to perdition.

Shāfiᶜī's antidote science was what he understood as *uṣūl al-dīn,* the fundamentals of religion—religion in the sense of obedience, *dīn,* obedience to God. To a theology of God Himself he opposed a theology of God's obligations for man to perform, leading man to his salvation. To the philosophical theology of the Muᶜtazila, Shāfiᶜī opposed his juridical theology, which is, in effect, a theology of praxis, a moral theology. In Shāfiᶜī's *Risāla* there is no legal philosophy, no philosophical theology.[6] That his work had instant success, one need not merely judge by the amazed admiration of Ibn Mahdī on turning over the pages of the work he had asked Shāfiᶜī to write.[7] There

[3]Shāfiᶜī, *ar-Risāla,* edited with introduction and annotation by Aḥmad Muḥammad Shākir (Cairo: al-Ḥalabī Press, 1358/1940).

[4]Ibn Taimīya, *Maᶜārij al-wuṣūl ilā maᶜrifat anna uṣūl ad-dīn wa-furūᶜahū qad baiyanahā ʾr-rasūl* (Cairo: al-Muʾaiyad Press, 1318/1900).

[5]See G. Makdisi, "The Juridical Theology of Shāfiᶜī: Origins and Significance of *Uṣūl al-Fiqh*" (in press).

[6]Cf. J. Schacht, *The Origins of Muhammadan Jurisprudence* (Oxford: Clarendon Press, 1950), p. 134.

[7]Ibn al-ᶜImād, *Shadharāt adh-dhahab fī akhbār man dhahab* (8 vols.; Cairo: al-Qudsī Press, 1350/1931), II, 10, ll. 11–13. For a biographical notice on Ibn Mahdī, see ibid., I, 355.

is a more telling indicator of the work's far-reaching significance: the swiftness with which the Muᶜtazila moved to infiltrate this newly constituted field of religious studies, injecting into it several problems of great ethical importance, questions that demanded answers, questions regarding which there is complete silence in Shāfiᶜī's *Risāla*.[8]

The Muᶜtazila held that good and evil are determined by the natural reason alone; supernatural revelation merely corroborates reason. On the other hand, the Ahl al-Hadith, or Traditionalists, believed that good and evil are known through revelation. To this the Muᶜtazila said: What about the qualification of acts before the advent of the revealed law (*ḥukm al-afᶜāl qabl wurūd ash-sharᶜ*)? This is one of several problems with which ūṣūl al-fiqh, the theory and methodology of the law, was henceforth to be concerned, among them the following: (1) the relation between reason and revelation (*al-ᶜaql wa'sh-sharᶜ, al-ᶜaql wa'n-naql, al-maᶜqūl wa'l-manqūl*); (2) the determination of good and evil (*at-taḥsīn wa't-taqbīḥ*); (3) prohibition and permission (*al-ḥaẓr wa'l-ibāḥa*); and (4) obligation beyond man's capacity (*taklīf mā lā yuṭāq*). After Shāfiᶜī these and other problems became part and parcel of the science of uṣūl al-fiqh, treated in the works of Rationalist, and many Traditionalist, writers.

Once these problems were brought to light, uṣūl al-fiqh had to deal with them; for in "the roots of law" were to be found the "roots of obligation." Islamic law is a divine positive law, consisting essentially of God's commands and prohibitions. It is mainly characterized by voluntarism: Acts are good or evil because God willed them so. Voluntarism was not unknown to the Christian West, both before and after St. Thomas Aquinas, to whom it was blasphemy. Peter Damian (1007–1072), a contemporary of Abū Yaᶜlā (d. 458/1066),[9] was an extremist theological voluntarist. Dazzled by divine omnipotence, he declared that God could make true even those things that reason considered absurd. For Damian, truth depended on God's will. And after St. Thomas, Duns Scotus (1266–1308) and William of Ockham (before 1300–ca. 1350) declared that action, to be good, must be commanded by God, and to be evil, must be forbidden by Him. The great Thomist philosopher, the late Jacques Maritain, was right in linking these two Christian theologians to theologians in Islam. In his book on *Moral Philosophy*—the subject of his seminar in Princeton in 1949–1950—at the end of Chapter Five in which he deals with "The Impact of Christianity on Moral Philosophy," Maritain speaks of a certain line of thinkers

[8] Early Muᶜtazili writings on uṣūl al-fiqh are known chiefly through excerpts cited in later works.

[9] On Abū Yaᶜlā, see G. Makdisi, *Ibn ᶜAqīl et la résurgence de l'Islam traditionaliste au XIe siècle* (Damascus: Institut Français de Damas, 1963), pp. 410 ff.; for his work on theology, see Abū Yaᶜlā, *al-MuᶜAamad fī uṣūl ad-dīn,* edited, translated, with introduction and notes by Wadīᶜ Z. Ḥaddād (Beirut: Dar el-Machreq, 1974).

> who, struck more or less consciously by the image of the revelation of the Decaloque amid the lightning and thunder of omnipotence, believed that the moral law, and finally even the distinction between good and evil, depended not at all on divine Wisdom and Reason, the foundation of eternal necessities, but uniquely and exclusively on the pure Will or the pure All-Powerfulness of God, and on an arbitrary decision of His sovereign Freedom. A kind of divine despotism thus became the source of the moral law, decreed and imposed without reason by the celestial High Command.[10]

Maritain included in this line of thinkers "the teachers of Islam above all, but also, on the Christian side, Scotus and Ockham in the Middle Ages. . . ."[11]

On the whole, Maritain's judgment is correct, but it should be nuanced in the case of Islam. "The teachers of Islam" were not *all* of this opinion: The Muᶜtazila are the first to come to mind as an important exception in this regard. But other exceptions must also be made even within the strictly Traditionalist camp, as, for instance, in the case of Ibn Taimīya's thought, in contradistinction to that of Ashᶜarī and other Muslim thinkers. Duns Scotus asserted the absolute freedom of God, but did not imply that God could act capriciously, as Ashᶜarī and others did. For Duns Scotus, divine acts have as their norm divine nature which, in its very essence, is rational. It is true, however, that outside of the Muᶜtazili movement and those among the Sunni and Shiᶜi thinkers who were influenced by it, the will of God is the ultimate source of morality. It is God who indicates what is good and what is evil; and good and evil are the conditions of moral obligation—*taklīf.*

Much of the best in Ibn Taimīya's thought is expressed in his work, *Minhāj as-Sunna.* The full title of this work in translation is "The Manifest Way of the Prophetic Tradition in Refutation of the Teachings of the Shīᶜa and Qadarīya."[12] For Ibn Taimīya, this last term, "al-Qadarīya," represents two antithetical theological schools of thought. One of these schools he calls also "al-Qadarīya al-mujbara" and, on occasion, "al-Jabrīya," whose ranks are made up of Jahmis and Ashᶜaris; the other school, to which he refers also as "al-ᶜAdlīya," is made up especially of Muᶜtazilis, philosophers, and Shiᶜis. Ibn Taimīya censures the first school for sacrificing divine justice to divine omnipotence; and the other, for sacrificing God's power to His justice. Ibn Taimīya's own doctrine is directed towards a middle ground in an effort to reconcile the two divine attributes.[13] In the *Minhāj,* Ibn Taimīya

[10] J. Maritain, *Moral Philosophy: An Historical and Critical Survey of the Great Systems* (New York: C. Scribner's Sons, 1964), p. 91, ll. 4 ff.

[11] Ibid., ll. 2–3.

[12] Ibn Taimīya, *Minhāj as-sunna an-nabawīya fi naqḍ kalām ash-Shīᶜa wa 'l-qadarīya* (4 vols.; Cairo: Būlāq, 1321–22/1903–04).

[13] See H. Laoust, *Essai sur les doctrines sociales et politiques de Taḳī-D-Dīn Aḥmad b. Taimīya* (Cairo: Institut Français d'Archéologie Orientale, 1939), pp. 165–166.

wrote in refutation of his contemporary, the Shiᶜi theologian al-Ḥillī, who, no doubt, influenced him by forcing him to rethink certain problems and give some answers to them.

According to Ḥillī, the Shiᶜi Imamis profess that God is just and wise; that He does not do evil, does not break a promise; that He acts for a purpose, does not act unjustly or in vain; that He is compassionate and merciful toward His creatures; does what is best and most beneficial for them; assigns them responsibilities to be performed voluntarily, not against their will; that He promises to reward them and threatens to punish them through His prophets who are infallible, inasmuch as it is not possible for them to err, nor to forget, nor to commit sins; otherwise, it would not be possible to put faith in their words or deeds, and their prophetic mission would be of no use; and so on. The Sunnis, according to Ḥillī, hold views in opposition to all of the foregoing tenets. They do not acknowledge justice or rationale in God's acts; they allow that God does evil and fails to fulfill His promises; that He acts for no purpose, unjustly and in vain; that He does not do what is best for His creatures; that the obedient among them are not rewarded; that the Prophets are not infallible; and so on. After listing these allegations of Ḥillī's, Ibn Taimīya states that such a representation of Sunni doctrines is false and distorted, and he sets out to answer them point by point at great length.[14]

After treating these problems, Ibn Taimīya points out that his opponent, al-Ḥillī, confines himself to quoting statements which he attributes to the generality of Sunni intellectuals, unaware that they apply to Ashᶜarī in particular. For these statements come to Ḥillī, says Ibn Taimīya, not from his Shiᶜi professors, but rather from the disciplies of Abū ᶜAlī al-Jubbā'ī, Abū Hāshim, Abū 'l-Ḥusain al-Baṣrī, and others, all of whom were Muᶜtazilis who wrote what they did in refutation of Sunni intellectuals in general, but of Ashᶜarī in particular.[15]

One of Ashᶜarī's often quoted doctrines is that of *kasb,* or *iktisāb,* a term usually translated as "acquisition."[16] Man "acquires" the responsibility of his acts, even though, according to Ashᶜarī, man's power to perform his acts is not his own. Man has no power over his own acts, the power to perform

[14] Ibn Taimīya, *Minhāj,* I, 30 ff.

[15] Ibid., I, 128, ll. 19 ff.

[16] The verbs *kasaba* (Form I) and *iktasaba* (Form VIII) occur in various conjugations in the Koran, to the exclusion of the infinitive nouns *kasb* and *iktisāb;* see M. F. ᶜAbd al-Bāqī, *al-Muᶜjam al-mufahras li-alfāẓ al-Qurʾān al-karīm* (Cairo: Dār al-Kutub Press, 1364/1945), pp. 604–605. On the doctrine of acquisition, see *Encyclopedia of Islam* (1st ed.; 1913–38), art. *kasb* (by D. B. Macdonald) and the bibliography there cited; al-Ashᶜarī, *Kitāb al-Lumaᶜ*, in R. J. McCarthy, *The Theology of al-Ashᶜarī* (Beirut: Imprimerie Catholique, 1953), Index, s.v. *kasb, iktisāb,* esp. Chapter V, pp. 37 ff. (Arabic text), 53 ff. (English translation); P. Boneschi, "*Kasaba* et *iktasaba:* leur acception figurée dans le Qurʾān," *Rivista degli studi*

them is God's; but man acquires responsibility for them. It is God who sets in motion the habitual existence in man of a power and a choice, so that He causes to exist in man the decreed act simultaneously with that power and that choice. Man's act is thus created by God and "acquired" by man. What is meant by man's acquisition is its simultaneity with man's power and will, without there being any influence from him or any participation in the existence of the act, other than his being a receptacle for it. In short, man's direction of his power and will towards the act is "acquisition"; and God's causing the act to exist after that is creation. What is meant by man's direction of his power is the making of it to be connected with the act, and that direction occurs through the link between the will and the act, not in the sense of an effective cause in the occurrence of that direction, for there is no cause but God; but rather in the sense that the connection of the will becomes a habitual means through which God creates in man a power connected with the act. Thus the one act is the result of God's power by way of bringing it into existence, and the result of man's power by way of acquiring it; the one object of power may be subject to two powers in two different ways.

This is how the doctrine of acquisition was explained in Tahānawī's *Kashshāf iṣṭilāḥāt al-funūn,*[17] who had relied upon Jurjānī's (d. 816/1463) *Commentary* on the *Mawāqif* or *Ījī* (d. 756/1355) and the *Commentary* on the latter's *ʿAqā'id* (perhaps by his disciple Muḥammad b. Hindūshāh ad-Dāmaghānī [fl. 778/1376]), and the glossaries.

The statement goes on to say that the Predestinarians (Jabrīya) assert that the cause of man's acts is God's power; man has no power at all,

---

*orientali,* 30 (1955), 17–53; A. J. Wensinck, *The Muslim Creed* (Cambridge: The University Press, 1932), Index, s.v. *kasb, iktisāb;* W. M. Watt, "The Origin of the Islamic Doctrine of Acquisition," *Journal of the Royal Asiatic Society* (1943), pp. 234–247; idem, *Free Will and Predestination in Early Islam* (London: Luzac, 1945), s.v. *kasb, iktisāb;* L. Gardet and M. M. [= G. C.] Anawati, *Introduction à la théologie musulmane: Essai de théologie comparée,* Etudes de Philosophie Médiévale, 37 (Paris: J. Vrin, 1948), Index, s.v. *kasb;* L. Gardet, *Les grands problèmes de la théologie musulmane: Dieu et la destinée de l'homme* (Paris: J. Vrin, 1967), pp. 60–64; M. Schwarz, "Acquisition (*kasb*) in Early Kalam," in S. M. Stern, Albert Hourani, and Vivian Brown, eds., *Essays Presented to Richard Walzer: Islamic Philosophy and the Classical Tradition* (Oxford: Bruno Cassirer Publ. Ltd., 1972), pp. 355–387; W. M. Watt, *The Formative Period of Islamic Thought* (Edinburgh: University Press, 1973), Index, s.v. *ksb; Encyclopedia of Islam* (2d ed.; 1954– ), Vol. IV, fascs. 71–72 (1976), art. *kasb* (by L. Gardet) and bibliography; on Qadi Abū Yaʿlā's use of the Ashʿarī concept of *kasb,* see D. Gimaret, "Théories de l'acte humain dans l'école hanbalite," *Bulletin d'Etudes Orientales,* 29 (1977), 157–178, esp. p. 163; idem, *Théories de l'acte humain en théologie musulmane,* Etudes Musulmanes, 24 (Paris: J. Vrin, 1980), Index, s.v. *kasb.*

[17]Tahānawī, *Kashshāf iṣṭilāḥāt al-funūn,* M. W. Abdalhaqq and G. Kadir under superintendence of A. Sprenger and W. N. Lees (2 vols.; Calcutta, 1854–62), s.v. *ksb.*

neither creative nor acquisitive; rather he is like inanimate beings. Al-Ashᶜarī says: The effective cause is God's power, but man has an acquisition of the act without any effect upon it. Most of the Muᶜtazila say: Man's acts occur through man's power alone, independently, not through necessary determination, but through choice.

Ibn Taimīya's doctrine of secondary causes comes in his discussion of God's creation in answer to one of Ḥillī's statements. Ḥillī had said that the teaching of the Sunni doctors leads to the assertion that God acts unjustly and unresponsibly. Ibn Taimīya counters by saying that there is no one among the adherents of Islam who says that God does what amounts to injustice on His part, or that He acts unresponsibly. Rather, those among the Sunnis and the Shiᶜis who affirm that God is the Creator of all things say that He created the acts of men, since these acts belong to the totality of things created. Among these created things there are those that are unjust on the part of their agents, but not on the part of their Creator.[18]

This is where Ibn Taimīya explains the distinction between the *agent* and the *Creator* in what amounts to the affirmation of secondary causes. He goes on to say that when God creates the act of man which is fasting, He Himself does not do the fasting; when He creates man's hunger and thirst, He Himself is not hungry or thirsty. The same is true when He creates the act of circumambulation, or genuflection and prostration in prayer, it is not He who circumambulates, genuflects, and prostrates. In short, when God creates an attribute or an act in a receptacle, neither the attribute nor the act is attributed to Himself; for if that were true, every contingent that He has created would be attributed to Him.[19]

When an attribute subsists in a receptacle, its qualification relates to that receptacle, not to any other. So, when God creates a motion in a receptacle, it is that receptacle that moves by virtue of that motion, not He who created the motion. The same applies to a color, or an odor, or to knowledge, or power, which God creates in a receptacle: It is that receptacle that is colored by virtue of that color, that exhales that odor, that knows by virtue of that knowledge, and so on.[20]

According to Ashᶜarī, says Ibn Taimīya, no act subsists in God; creation is none other than the thing created (*al-khalq huwa 'l-makhlūq*); and this is also the opinion of a group of jurisconsults of the schools of Mālik, Shāfiᶜī, and Aḥmad.[21] By saying that God creates the acts of men, Ashᶜarī was forced to conclude that the acts of men were God's acts, for, according to him, *the doing* of God is the same as *the thing done* (*fiᶜluhū huwa mafᶜūluh*). Ashᶜarī did not say that the acts of men were their own acts except by metaphor

[18] Ibn Taimīya, *Minhāj,* I, 126, ll. 17 ff.

[19] Ibid., ll. 20 ff.

[20] Ibid., ll. 28 ff.

[21] Ibid., I, 127, ll. 2–3.

(*ʿalā wajhi 'l-majāz*); what he said was that they were men's "acquisitions"; and he explained "acquisition" as that which occurs in the receptacle of contingent power in conjunction with it.[22]

Ashʿarī, says Ibn Taimīya elsewhere in his *Minhāj,* affirms for man a contingent power and choice when he says that the act is man's acquisition; but he also says that man's power has no effect on bringing the object of power into existence. This is why people have said that Ashʿarī's acquisition is inconceivable. But the generality of Ahl al-Ithbāt[23] say that man is truly the agent of his act, that he is endowed with power and choice, a power that has an effect on its object.[24]

The basic difference between Ibn Taimīya and al-Ashʿarī, with regard to human acts, consists in the fact that, for Ibn Taimīya, man is truly the efficient cause of his own acts: God is the Creator (*al-khāliq*), and man is the agent (*al-fāʿil*). For Ashʿarī, man is not the efficient cause of his own acts; that is, God is the Creator as well as the Agent of human acts; but man "acquires" the responsibility for his acts: He somehow gets saddled with the responsibility for acts of which he is not the agent.

It should be noted, however, that Ashʿarī's thought is not easy to pin down. Ibn Taimīya himself points out that while Ashʿarī holds to the opinion first described, he has also been known to opt for the opposing opinion.[25] Ibn Taimīya does not, to my knowledge, indicate where Ashʿarī expounds such a thesis, and this is not necessarily due to Ibn Taimīya's lack of direct knowledge of Ashʿarī's works. In reference to the divine attributes Ibn Taimīya refers to a doctrine, saying that "Ashʿarī stated that in most of his works, such as the *Mūjaz, al-Maqālāt al-kabīr, al-Maqālāt aṣ-ṣaghīr, al-Ibāna,* and others, and his statements regarding the question did not change."[26] Elsewhere he cites Ashʿarī's *Risāla ilā ahl ath-thaghr,* in which Ashʿarī censures the Muʿtazila on a matter later taken up by Imām al-Ḥaramain al-Juwainī.[27] Elsewhere again he cites two works of Ashʿarī's, the *Lumaʿ* and the above-mentioned *Risāla ilā ahl ath-thaghr,* describing the theology that

[22] Ibid., ll. 8 ff.; see also Ibn Taimīya, *Kitāb an-Nubūwāt* (Cairo: al-Munīrīya Press, 1346/1928), p. 97, ll. 8 ff.

[23] The term *Ahl al-Ithbāt* (literally: "The People of Affirmation") has been variously applied to Muʿtazilis, Ashʿaris, and Traditionalists, the doctors usually claiming it for the group to which they belong. Cf. Watt, *Free Will and Predestination in Early Islam,* pp. 55 f., 112 f.; D. Gimaret, *Théories,* pp. 62 ff., 70 ff., et passim.

[24] Ibid., II, 16 (penult.)–17, ll. 1–3.

[25] Ibn Taimīya, *Minhāj,* I, 127, l. 17: "ammā sā'ir Ahl as-Sunna fa-yaqūlūna inna afʿāla 'l-ʿibādi fiʿlun la-hum haqīqatan, *wa-huwa aḥadu 'l-qaulaini li 'l-Ashʿarī.*"

[26] Ibid., I, 204: "wa-qad dhakara 'l-Ashʿarī dhālika fī ʿāmmati kutubih, ka 'l-Mūjaz, . . . , wa-lam yakhtalif fī dhālika kalāmuh."

[27] Ibn Taimīya says here that, in his *Risāla,* "Ashʿarī shows that such was not one of the methods followed by the prophets . . ."; see Ibn Taimīya, *Bayān muwāfaqat ṣarīḥ al-maʿqūl li-ṣaḥīḥ al-manqūl* (on the margins of Ibn Taimīya's *Minhāj*) (4 vols.; Cairo: Būlāq, 1321–22/1903–04), II, 96, ll. 27–29.

Ashᶜarī elaborates in these two works;[28] he states categorically that Ashᶜarī, in agreement with the Muᶜtazila, follows a thesis of the Jahmīya "in all of his works."[29]

The classical Ashᶜarī doctrine of God as both Creator and Agent of human acts, and of man as the "acquirer" of responsibility for them, is based on Ashᶜarī's *Lumaᶜ*,[30] and is the doctrine which survives in Ashᶜarī tradition, as already described;[31] outstanding exceptions to this tradition are Imām al-Ḥaramain al-Juwainī and Fakhr ad-Dīn ar-Rāzī.

Having asserted man's influence over his own acts, that he truly brings the act into existence by virtue of a power of which God is the Creator and man the agent, and that man's voluntary acts are according to his own intentions, Ibn Taimīya avoids Ashᶜarī's doctrine which undermines the moral issue of responsibility, holding man responsible for acts over which he has no effective power, acts not of his own doing.

This brings us to the problem of the determination of good and evil. To this central problem in moral theology, Ibn Taimīya tells us that he devoted a separate work which, unfortunately, has not come down to us.[32] But he does discuss the problem here and there in his extant works, in the *Minhāj as-Sunna* in refutation of the Shiᶜa and Muᶜtazila, and in *Bayān muwāfaqat ṣarīḥ al-maᶜqūl li-ṣaḥīḥ al-manqūl,*[33] a work on the reconciliation of reason and revelation. Some of Ibn ᶜAqīl's ideas on the subject may be found in his intellectual diary, the *Kitāb al-Funūn;*[34] his work on theology, *Kitāb al-Irshād,* is still lost. We do have a separate work devoted to this subject by a Hanbali jurisconsult and theologian, aṭ-Ṭūfī, a contemporary of Ibn Taimīya. It is entitled *Darᵓ al-qabīḥ fī ᵓt-taḥsīn waᵓ t-taqbīḥ* (The Warding Off of Evil in the Determination of Good and Evil) and has survived in one manuscript in Istanbul.[35] From these three sources we should be able to get some idea of Hanbali thought on the subject as compared with that of Ashᶜarī and the Ashᶜaris.

[28] Ibn Taimīya, *Kitāb an-Nubūwāt,* p. 49, ll. 7 ff.

[29] Ibid., p. 53 (ult.): "salakahā 'l-Ashᶜarī fī kutubihī kullihā mutābaᶜatan li 'l-Muᶜtazila." See also Ibn Taimīya, *Bayān,* II, 9, where he refers to "all of the books" of Ashᶜarī and names the *Ibāna,* the *Mūjaz,* and the *Maqālāt,* to which latter work he frequently refers and from which he quotes; see *Minhāj,* I, 214, 265, and *Bayān,* II, 14.

[30] See n. 16 above.

[31] See n. 17 above.

[32] Ibn Taimīya, *Minhāj,* III, 31: "wa-laisa 'l-maqṣūdu 'l-kalāma fī 't-taḥsīni wa 't-taqbīḥi 'l-ᶜaqlī; fa-qad takallamnā ᶜalaihī fī ghairi hādhā 'l-mauḍiᶜ fī *muṣannafin mufrad.*"

[33] See n. 27 above.

[34] Ibn ᶜAqīl, *Kitāb al-Funūn,* 2 parts, ed. G. Makdisi, Série I: Pensée Arabe et Musulmane, vols. 44 and 45 (Beirut: Institut de Lettres Orientales, 1970–1971).

[35] A study of this work is now in progress, and I hope to submit it to the press in the near future.

Ibn ᶜAqīl expresses his opinion on the subject in his report of a disputation taking place between a Traditionalist and a Muᶜtazili Rationalist, excerpts of which are given here. The Traditionalist gives his opinion as follows:

> Our basic principle is that reason neither permits nor prohibits. If the revealed law does not come with permission and prohibition, the means of arriving at them are impossible. If the means are impossible, there can be no way to issuing a legal opinion [*fatwā, responsum*] one way or another, for the only way left to us then would be conjecture and surmise, and that method is not acceptable for God's precepts.[36]

To this the Muᶜtazili objected, saying:

> I do not concede this principle. On the contrary, reason has its judgments to make, and among these are permission and prohibition. . . . And we can quote statements of intellectuals in support of what we hold to be true. And that is that there is consensus among them that in the revealed law there is nothing that is contrary to reason. . . . If reason could not distinguish between good and evil, how would we be able to recognize God's admonitions and exhortations?[37]

That this answer of the Muᶜtazili fairly represents the opinion of Ibn ᶜAqīl is made clear in one of Ibn ᶜAqīl's academic sermons, a summary of which follows:

> If the knowledge of good and evil through reason did not precede our knowledge of the revealed laws, the revelation's severe reprimand and censure for an act would not be possible. They would be possible only if there is in the revealed law a prior command to perform an act, but the act was avoided; or a prior prohibition of it but it was performed. When God said: "Worship ye that which ye yourselves do carve?" (37, 95); "Will ye cry unto Baal and forsake the best of Creators?" (37, 125). "And the People of Moses, after (he had left them), chose a calf (for worship), (made) out of their ornaments; it seemed to low: did they not see that it could neither speak to them nor show them the way?" (7, 148). All of the Koran's censures are apprehended through reason; thus the revealed law censured those endowed with reason in which there is a prior knowledge of good and evil. And God said: "Bethink you: If the revelation is from God and ye reject it—who is further astray than one in open feud (with the Lord)?" (41, 52). This is censure for neglecting precaution against harm, and this belongs to the judgments of reason.

[36] Ibn ᶜAqīl, *Kitāb al-Funūn,* p. 400, ll. 2 ff.

[37] Ibid., pp. 400, l. 7–401, e. 10.

> And God said: "If he is lying, then the lie is upon him; and if he is truthful, then some of that wherewith he threateneth you will strike you" (40, 28). All of these Koranic verses call for the taking of precautions; and nothing but reason can perform this function.[38]

Reason has a prior knowledge of what is good and what is evil. Reason has judgments to make. The Koran addresses reason, points out that precaution is needed; and precaution is a function performed by reason.

In the following passage, Ibn ᶜAqīl reports a disputation between an Ashᶜari and a Muᶜtazili. The Ashᶜari is quoted as follows:

> How is it possible for a reasonable man to trust his reason when, before the revelation, he knows if he considered the pain inflicted on an animal, and the destruction of its body (when slaughtered), he would judge the act of slaughter to be evil. The same judgment would apply to the kissing of attractive youths, to the wearing of silk in winter, to the listening to songstresses and their music—he would judge all this to be good, because of the good it would bring to body and soul. But with the advent of the revealed laws all of these things were foresaken; and not only do we slaughter animals, we do so as a means of drawing closer to God by performing the deed as a religious sacrifice. Therefore, the reasonable man does not pass judgment according to the dictates of reason; nor does he declare a thing to be evil because reason so declares it; he entrusts the matter to the revealed law.[39]

A Muᶜtazili in the gathering answers him, saying:

> This argument of yours, is it good or bad? If you say "good," or if you say "bad," we shall then ask you how you arrived at your determination of it either way. If you say, "through reason," that would be enough to annul what you have determined. If you say, "I know this through the revealed law," you shall be asked, "Where is the text in Koran or Sunna in support of your statement?"
>
> But I'll give you more room to move in, so that you don't feel cramped, and ask you: Do you think that causing pain to the animal by slaughtering it was considered good, after its determination by reason as bad, simply because it was painful? Certainly not! But we know through reason the wisdom of the Legislator (= God), and that He would neither do evil, nor legislate the doing of evil. If we allowed this as possible, we would no longer have any way of knowing the veracity of God's messengers. But since we already know that the Eternal Maker is wise and does not do evil, we are certain that He would not endorse a liar. It is

[38] Ibid., pp. 648, l. 14–649, l. 9.
[39] Ibid., pp. 548, l. 13–549, l. 5.

> therefore certain that since He endorses certain persons through their performance of miracles, they are truthful. This being the case, when the revealed laws provide for the causing of pain to animals, we know that it must be for a good underlying cause, or some welfare. Moreover, reason does not consider all causes of pain, without exception, to be evil. On the contrary, the slitting of an abcess, the pain of phlebotomy and cupping, the ingestion of distasteful medicines, all of this causes pain; so also the punishments used in order to discourage evil deeds. All this is good, since it leads to the welfare of what is more worthy, and to the preservation of the whole. The causing of pain which is endorsed by the revealed law is of this category. But as for the pain caused for no good underlying reason, certainly not![40]

The disputation ends on this note, and Ibn ᶜAqīl says that the Ashᶜari was nonplussed.[41]

Agreeing with Ibn ᶜAqīl is a famous disciple of Ibn Taimīya, the jurisconsult and Sufi Ibn Qaiyim al-Jauzīya who, in his *Miftāḥ dār as-saᶜāda* (The Key to the House of Happiness), asserts that reason knows the distinction between good and evil prior to the promulgation of the revealed law, and independently of it. Ethical values are not based exclusively on the law, but also on reason; otherwise, he says, there would be no basis for reasoning by analogy.[42]

As Ibn Taimīya differs from Ashᶜarī on the structure of human acts, he also differs from him on the problem of the determination of good and evil. He broaches the subject while answering one of the accusations made by his Shiᶜi contemporary, al-Ḥillī. Ḥillī had accused the Sunnis of attributing evil to God and implying that God does not fulfill his promises. Ibn Taimīya denies this of any group of Muslims. He then takes this opportunity to fling back at the Muᶜtazila, and at those Shiᶜa who agree with them, Ḥillī included, the accusation of anthropomorphism. They deny divine omnipotence, he says, and impose upon God the same obligations and prohibitions as on men, instituting for God a law similar to that of men. They are therefore the "assimilationists of acts" (*mushabbihat al-afᶜāl*), meaning that they are guilty of anthropomorphism regarding the acts of God, assimilating them to those of men. Sunnis and Shiᶜis who affirm the reality of divine omnipotence are in agreement that God cannot be compared in His acts to His creatures. They also agree that what God has promised His creatures will necessarily occur by virtue of His promise, for He is truthful and never fails to keep His promises.[43]

[40] Ibid., pp. 549, l. 6–550, l. 4.

[41] Ibid., p. 550, l. 4.

[42] Ibn Qaiyim al-Jauzīya, *Miftāḥ dār as-saᶜāda wa-manshūr wilāyat al-ᶜilm wa ʾl-irāda* (2 vols.; Cairo: al-Khānjī Press, 1323/1905), II, 45.

[43] Ibn Taimīya, *Minhāj,* I, 124.

Ibn Taimīya then says that Muslims, both Sunnis and Shiʿis, differ among themselves on the problem of the determination of good and evil according to two opinions. The first opinion is that of Ashʿarī and his followers, and also of many jurisconsults of the Maliki, Shafiʿi, and Hanbali schools. According to this opinion, good and evil may not be known through reason, but only through revelation.

Opposed to this is the second opinion, according to which good and evil may be known through reason. Ibn Taimīya then points out that though this opinion is generally known to be that of the Muʿtazila, it is also that of several other groups, namely, the Karramiya, the generality of Hanafi jurisconsults, and many jurisconsults of the Maliki, Shafiʿi, and Hanbali schools. Ibn Taimīya cites specifically the Maliki Abharī, the Shafiʿis Ibn Abī Huraira, and al-Qaffāl, and, without naming them, certain groups of Traditionalist masters. He also cites by name two Hanbali jurisconsults, Abū ʾl-Ḥasan at-Tamīmī and Abū ʾl-Khaṭṭāb (al-Kalwadhānī), adding that Kalwadhānī (who was a contemporary of Ibn ʿAqīl) stated that this opinion was also that of most of the ulama. Ibn Taimīya goes on to say that the advocates of this second opinion considered those who advocated the first opinion, Ashʿarī and the others, to belong to Ahl al-bidaʿ, the heretical innovators. This was stated explicitly in the *Risāla fī ʾs-sunna* (The Epistle on Orthodoxy) of the eleventh-century Abū Naṣr as-Sijzī, a well-known work in Ibn Taimīya's day, as well as in its *Commentary, Qaṣīda fī's-sunna* (Ode on Orthodoxy), by his disciple Abū ʾl-Qāsim Saʿd b. ʿAlī az-Zanjānī (d. ca. 470/1178). Both authors were Shafiʿis.[44]

Ibn Taimīya, in this passage, does not say to which of the two opinions he adheres, but it is clear that he is in sympathy with the advocates of reason as the source for determining good and evil. That he favors this opinion is made explicit in another passage, in connection with the legal qualifications of acts. The truth of the matter, he says, is that the legal qualifications of acts do not belong to the category of necessary attributes, rather they are accidental attributes applying to acts in accordance with whether they are to be done or avoided. Good and evil are understood in the sense of a thing being desirable or reprehensible, beneficial or harmful, and so on. They are real attributes of the things qualified, varying with variations of circumstances, but are not their necessary attributes. To say that acts have no attributes requiring the qualification of good or evil would be like saying that bodies have no properties enabling them to heat or cool, to satifsy hunger or quench thirst; thus to negate the properties of substances which necessitate their effects is like negating the qualifications of acts necessitating their effects.

Ibn Taimīya goes on to say that the generality of Muslims who affirm the natures and properties of substances, affirm also the good and evil in acts

[44] Ibid., I, 124–125.

with respect to their being done or avoided. He then quotes the following Koranic verse (7, 157): "He commands them that which is right and prohibits them that which is wrong. He allows them as lawful what is good and forbids them what is bad." This indicates, he says, that an act in itself is right or wrong, and that food is good or bad. And this is where Ibn Taimīya makes clear his opinion that good and evil are not dependent upon command and prohibition. He says: If there were no qualities in substances or acts except by virtue of their connection with commands and prohibitions, the implied meaning of the Koranic verse would be, "He commands them what He commands them and forbids them what He forbids them, and He allows them as lawful what He allows them as lawful and forbids them what He forbids them." But, says Ibn Taimīya, God is far above this kind of discourse.[45]

This opinion is corroborated in another work of Ibn Taimīya's in which he states that acts have qualifications necessitating their being good and obligatory, or evil and prohibited, and that those qualifications as good or evil may be known through reason (*wa-anna dhalika yuᶜlamu bi 'l-ᶜaql*); but God does not inflict punishment on anyone in the Hereafter, except after the prophetic message has reached him. Here he quotes the Koranic verse: "Nor would we visit with our wrath until We had sent an apostle (to give warning)." Ibn Taimīya says that Ashᶜarī and his followers, and those doctors who agree with them, such as Qadi Abū Yaᶜlā and his followers, allow that God may inflict punishment even on those who are free of sin. They even go so far as to say that God may punish innocent children in the Hereafter.[46]

It should be pointed out that, on the problem of good and evil, it is possible to find one and the same doctor giving one opinion in one place, and another opposing opinion in another place. In such a case it is possible that he may have changed his mind at a later date, in which case a study of the chronology of his works may yield, of the two opposing opinions, the one upon which he finally settled. The difficulty here is that it is not always possible to establish such a chronology, either because of the loss of many of the given author's works, or because there are no clues to be found in his extant works which would make the chronology possible.

Ashᶜarī, even according to Ibn Taimīya, has two opposing opinions on the problem of good and evil. Ibn Taimīya himself is not always consistent. Ibn ᶜAqīl holds an opinion in his work on legal theory and methodology which is opposed to that already quoted. After citing Tamīmī, of his own school, as being of the opinion that the determination of good and evil comes under the jurisdiction of reason, which agrees with his own opinion in *Kitāb al-Funūn,* Ibn ᶜAqīl states in his *Wāḍiḥ:*

[45] Ibid., II, 34, ll. 1–12.
[46] Ibn Taimīya, *Kitāb an-Nubūwāt,* p. 163, ll. 7–12.

> . . . but the opinion to be relied upon is that the revealed law determines good and evil, and that, in these matters, reason is not the judge, but rather is subject to the judgment of revelation. The proof for this, according to this book, which is on the fundamentals of law (*uṣūl al-fiqh*), not on the premises of theology (*uṣūl ad-dīn*), is that those who profess that reason determines evil are like the Brahmins, who declare that it is evil to cause pain to animals. . . .

The passage ends with this statement:

> . . . we have agreed that the Legislator (= God) causes pain not through need to do so, and that that is good. Therefore, the assertion that reason determines good and evil is false.[47]

Thus it would seem as though Ibn ʿAqīl held two diametrically opposed opinions on the subject of good and evil; but that is not the case. Islam, like Judaism and Christianity, has a catalogue of things forbidden and permitted, based on Scripture and tradition, and regarding which reason has nothing to say. The prohibitions of eating pork or abstaining from meat on certain days of the year are examples, in one or another of these religions, of religiously imposed sanctions where reason does not enter into the picture. But such negative considerations cannot constitute moral theology, because this would amount to a moral of the minimum. For Ibn Taimīya, this would not be enough; Muslim life itself is the scope of Muslim ethics. His criticism of certain Sufis was that they considered themselves above the law: The generality of men have one sort of morality to follow, and they, the elite, another. For this type of Sufi, law was but the starting point; for Ibn Taimīya, it was the point of arrival:[48] To love God is to love His commands, to obey Him in His commands and prohibitions, and beyond that, to perform supererogatory works.

Ibn ʿAqīl, in the *Wāḍiḥ,* sensing that the problem of good and evil is susceptible to misunderstanding and may lead to accusations of self-contradiction, makes some important distinctions:

> Note that all the known principles in matters of religion (*aḥkām ad-dīn*) are bound to belong to one of three divisions: one division can be known only through reason, to the exclusion of revelation; a second division cannot be known through reason, but only through revelation; and a third division which can be known through reason and through revelation.[49]

[47] Ibn ʿAqīl, *al-Wāḍiḥ fī uṣūl al-fiqh,* National Library of Damascus (Ẓāhirīya), MS. *uṣūl al-fiqh 78,* fol. 6a–6b.

[48] See Laoust, *Essai,* p. 472, n. 2.

[49] Ibn ʿAqīl, *al-Wāḍiḥ,* fol. 14b.

In the first division, Ibn ᶜAqīl lists questions that are found in the premisses of theology, such as the contingency of the world, the existence of its Creator, His unicity, His necessary attributes, the reality of the prophetic mission; in short, all that is connected with *tauḥīd* and *nubūwa*. In the second division, he lists all questions coming under the designation of law and legal theory and methodology: knowledge that the act of religious responsibility is good or bad, allowed or prohibited, an act of obedience or disobedience, obligatory or recommendable, a valid contract, a sound conveyance of property, and so on. In the third division, he includes every judgment or premiss of reason the ignorance of which does not prejudice knowledge of the unicity of God and the prophethood. For instance, knowledge of the possibility of seeing God with our eyes, the possibility of forgiveness for sinners other than the infidels, knowledge of the soundness of using the isolated tradition as a valid source of action, and reasoning by analogy to determine legal qualifications. The *mukallaf* (i.e., one obligated to observe the religious precepts) may be ignorant of these and other such matters, and still know God and the prophethood, despite his ignorance. It is clear that once reason establishes the truth of God's existence and the mission of His prophet, then the Sacred Scriptures, that is, the Koran and the sunna of the Prophet, form the basis of obligation—taklīf.[50]

The problem underlying that of the determination of good and evil is one of legitimacy—the legitimacy of the knowledge according to which this determination is to be decided. Is it to be decided on the basis of a philosophical theology, kalām, or on the basis of a juridical theology, uṣūl al-fiqh? This is not so much whether good and evil are determined by reason or revelation; rather, the question is whether this determination is to be made by reason unaided or by reason aided by the data of revelation. And it is this question that brings us to the crux of the problem: What are the fundamentals of religion (uṣūl ad-dīn)? Is uṣūl ad-dīn the kalām, or is it the Law? The question, put in these terms, brings us closer to understanding the conflict between Traditionalism and Rationalism.

Traditionalism does not necessarily deny the value of philosophical theology, any more than it denies the value of philosophy. It regards both as valuable when used in the defense of Islam—weapons used for a specific purpose: to protect the borders of Islam from invasion by the hostile forces of pagan or heretical thought. Within the borders, in the meantime, the work proceeds involving those efforts expended to the utmost limit, sometimes in philosophizing within the faith, but more often in the elaboration and application of the Law—that is to say, the elaboration and application, on earth, of God's commands and prohibitions.

[50] Ibid., fols. 14b–15a.

# LEGAL IMPLICATIONS FOR TODAY OF *AL-AḤKĀM AL-KHAMSA* (THE FIVE VALUES)

KEMAL FARUKI

S. M. Government Law College, Karachi

As an all-embracing system concerned with both the spiritual and the temporal, the collective and the personal, it is natural that Islam should seek to evaluate all human acts and relationships in terms of their moral beauty (*ḥusn*) or ugliness (*qubḥ*). This evaluation led in one important direction to a classification that found finished expression in the Five Values (*al-aḥkām al-khamsa*): "obligatory" (*wājib* or *farḍ*), "recommended" (*mandūb*), "permitted" or "indifferent" (*mubāḥ*), "disliked" (*makrūh*), and finally, "forbidden" (*ḥarām*).

The difference between the Five Values in terms of sanctions was that, if obligatory, the commission was rewarded and the omission punished; if recommended, the commission was rewarded but the omission was not punished; if permitted or indifferent, there was neither reward nor punishment for commission or omission; if disliked, there was no punishment if committed but there was reward if omitted; and finally, if forbidden, there was punishment for commission and reward for omission. We shall return later to the question of who was to administer the reward or punishment.

There was a lapse of some centuries before the Five Values settled into this form and there are some remarkable differences between their usage in early and in classical times to which we shall also return, but at the outset some important nuances should be noted.[1]

[1]This development with regard to mubah may be studied in al-Amidī (d. 631/1233), *al-Iḥkām fī Uṣūl al-Aḥkām* (Cairo, 1333/1914), I:176, and in Ibn ʿĀbidīn (d. 1252/1836), *Radd al-Muhtar ʿalā Durr al-Mukhtār* (Cairo, n.d.), III:251. On the development of the Five Values as a whole see also al-Jaṣṣāṣ (d. 370/980), *al-Aḥkām al-Qurʾān* (Istanbul, 1335/1916), II:169–170; Abū'l-Ḥussain M. b. ʿAlī b. al-Ṭayyib (d. 436/1044), *K. al-Muʿtamad fī Uṣūl al-Fiqh* (Damascus, 1384/1964), I:8; Imām al-Ḥarāmain al-Jūwainī (d. 478/1085), *al-Waraqa fī Uṣūl al-Fiqh,* in *Majmūmʿutūn Uṣūlīya* (Damascus, n.d.), p. 28; al-Shirāzī (d. 476/1083), *al-Lūmaʿ fī Uṣūl al-Fiqh* (Mecca, n.d.); and al-Ghazālī (d. 505/1111), *al-Mustaṣfāʿ* (Cairo, 1356/1937), I:42, 140, 170 and 176.

(1) Is the original condition one of permission (*ibāḥa*) with prohibition (*taḥrīm*) only when specifically stated, or is the original condition one of prohibition with permission requiring explicit assertion? The general view appears to have been that the basic condition is permission or liberty, but some thinkers took the view that the basic condition was one of prohibition.[2]

(2) Most obligatory acts are obligatory on an individual basis for each and every Muslim man and woman (*farḍ ʿayn*), but certain duties, such as attendance at funeral prayers, are adequately fulfilled if a sufficiency of Muslims are present (*farḍ kifāya*).

(3) The opposite of forbidden (ḥarām) is normally obligatory (wājib or farḍ), as they exist in the Five Values, it being obligatory to fast during the month of Ramaḍān and therefore forbidden to eat or drink between sunrise and sunset. But in another sense the opposite of forbidden is lawful (ḥalāl), it being forbidden to eat pig's meat but lawful to eat fruit. Here no sense of obligatory compulsion is implied in the lawfulness of eating fruit.

(4) Other phrases and words are used in the Qurʾān and in the ḥadīth compilations which seek to record the practice (*sunna*) of the Prophet Muhammad (o.w.b.p.) and are found also in the writings of the early jurists, for example, "it is prescribed" (*kutiba*) instead of wājib or farḍ, "good" (*ḥasan*) or "liked" (*mustaḥabb*) or "better" (*khair*) instead of mandūb, and "no harm" (*la baʾsa*) or "permissible" (*jāʾiz*) instead of mubāḥ, and so on.

(5) Other discussions by the jurists concern such matters as whether a particular act or relationship is forbidden intrinsically (*ḥarām lidhātihī*) or extrinsically (*ḥarām lighairihī*), that is, not because the act or relationship itself is bad but because it leads to something that is forbidden.[3]

(6) It should be borne in mind that under certain circumstances an act can move away from its normal value and even to its opposite value. For instance, pig's meat is normally forbidden, but it becomes virtually obligatory to eat it if the alternative is starving to death; and fasting in Ramaḍān is normally obligatory but is forbidden in certain types of illnesses or for infants.

(7) There are differences between the various Islamic schools of law regarding the value attached to a particular act. These differences are usually of degree, but on occasion are in striking contrast. Some examples are: The use of perfume on the body while wearing *iḥrām* for *ḥajj* is recommended by three of the Sunni schools but is disapproved of by the Malikis if the fragrance remains on the body; the sale of a woman's milk is forbidden according to the Hanafis but permissible according to the Shafis; sodomy

[2]The different views are summarized by Ibn ʿĀbidīn, *ar-Radd,* III:25, and by al-Amidī, *al-Iḥkām,* I:176.

[3]Two examples of ḥarām lighairihi are looking at a strange woman and doing any business after the *adhān* (call) to Friday prayers.

(*liwāṭa*) is equated with adultery by three Sunni schools, which prescribe the so-called "fixed" (*ḥadd*) punishment with the same evidential requirements as for adultery, but the Hanafis hold that the punishment is discretionary (*taʿzīr*) and only two witnesses are required.[4]

(8) The distinction should be kept in mind between the Five Values and the legal differences between "valid" (*ṣaḥīḥ*), "void" (*bāṭil*), and "irregular" (*fāsid*). This is illustrated in the case of marriage by a valid marriage which is correct in form and in substance, a void marriage such as one purportedly contracted between persons related within the prohibited degrees, and an irregular marriage where there is a defect in form which can be cured or which in any case preserves some of the consequences or benefits of a valid marriage such as one without the requisite number of witnesses.

It is clear that the Five Values bear an intimate relationship to Islamic law, and Islamic law, in turn, is a crucial element in the Islamic resurgence which appears to characterize so much of the Muslim world today. One might also assert that the enunciation of the Five Values has played an important part in molding the outlook of Muslims with respect to the quality of an act or relationship and the nature of the individual or community response that should be evoked.

The primary source for this value classification is, of course, the Qurʾān, followed closely by the known practice (sunna) of the Prophet, and later by the standard ḥadīth compilations made about two hundred years after the death of the Prophet, which sought to record the sunna of the Prophet.

When extracting values from these primary sources the early jurists were extremely cautious in expressing their opinions. They avoided dogmatic, uncompromising assertions. Thus we find terms such as "no harm" or "no good" or "I personally dislike" or "I personally prefer" much more frequently than outright orders and prohibitions. Where outright orders and prohibitions do occur, they are usually on matters of social significance or on matters for which direct explicit authority can be found in the Qurʾān.

The reason for this is brought out by Abū Yūsuf (d. 179/795), the immediate disciple of Abū Ḥanīfa (d. 150/767), in his observations on Auzāʿī (d. 158/774). Al-Auzāʿī was the founder of the Syrian school of law which later became extinct. It appears that he reacted strongly against the excessively worldly and pragmatic atmosphere of the Umayyad government in Damascus. In *Radd ʿalā Siyār al-Auzāʿī* Abū Yūsuf deprecates the immoderate use by al-Auzāʿī of the terms ḥalāl (lawful) and ḥarām (forbidden) as follows: "What a presumptuous statement of al-Auzāʿī is 'This is ḥalāl from God.' I found my teachers disliked the practice of saying in their decisions 'This is ḥalāl (lawful)' and 'This is ḥarām (forbidden)' except that

[4] An extensive examination of these differences is set out in ʿAbd Allāh M. b. ʿAbd ar-Raḥmān, *Raḥmat al-Umma fī Ikhtilāf al-Aʾimma* (Cairo, 1300/1882), I:17 ff.

which is expressly mentioned in the Qurʾān without any *tafsīr* (commentary)." In the same place Abū Yūsuf quotes an eminent successor (one of the second generation of Muslims) to the companions (those who became Muslims during the lifetime of the Prophet): "One should not say that 'God made it lawful' or 'liked it' because God would then say to such a person that He did not make it lawful nor did He like it. Similarly, one should not say that 'God made it ḥarām (forbidden)' for then God would say that he told a lie and that He did not make it unlawful nor did He forbid it." Abū Yūsuf then quotes Ibrāhīm al-Nakhaʾī (d. 95/713), probably the earliest of the speculative lawyers, to the same effect.[5]

There are three explanations for this approach. (1) The early jurists possessed a vivid awareness that justice will be accurately meted out on the Day of Reckoning. (2) They conceived of their task as being to help quicken the conscience of the believer. (3) They possessed a profound fear of being punished themselves if they attempted to arrogate for themselves the sole prerogatives of God on the Day of Judgment.

By classical times there was a far wider use of the concepts obligatory and forbidden. The state and society were legally empowered to intervene in a far larger range of matters, including many which seem, from a direct reading of the Qurʾān and much of ḥadīth, to pertain to questions of personal conscience and on which judgment was reserved for God on the Day of Reckoning, God the All-Knowing Who Alone can weigh such matters on the finest of fine balances.

A superficial assessment might conclude that there was a weaker awareness of, and confidence in, God's capacity or wish to intervene in human affairs in classical and postclassical times, and in the reality of the Day of Reckoning; but the real explanation for the change appears to be connected with the change in the distinction between the rights of (or duties towards) God (*ḥuqūq Allāh*) and the rights of (or duties towards) mankind (*ḥuqūq al-insān*) or, as they are also called, the rights of (or duties towards) God's slaves (*ḥuqūq al-ʿibād*). In early times, judging from the works of the jurists, whenever a pure right of God was infringed it was believed that God Himself would punish, and only when the rights of men were infringed could the state or society mete out punishment. The rights of God were the formal acts of worship—the confession of faith, prayer, alms-giving, fasting, and the pilgrimage—or of personal goodness seeking God's pleasure (*ʿibādāt*), while the rights of mankind concerned social transactions and relationships (*muʿāmalāt*) and penal sanctions (*ʿuqūbāt*).

The classical and postclassical notion that the state or society could punish any infraction of the rights of God seems to have appeared after the concept of the caliphate had been virtually transformed from the concept existing at

[5] Abū Yūsuf, *ar-Radd* (Cairo, n.d.), pp. 72–73.

the time of the first four Rightly Directed Caliphs (*al-khulafāʾ ar-rāshidūn*). The caliphate was declining in terms of the area it controlled and deriving less and less legitimacy and respect from the community at the very time it was threatened by the Persian Shiʿī Buyid and subsequent Turkish Sunni Seljuk occupations of Baghdad, the capital of the ʿAbbāsids. There was also the growing threat resulting from the Fāṭimid invasion from Cairo of Western Asia. Compensation was sought for this weakening by giving ever more purely theoretical authority to the caliph (and to the state) and by regarding him as the shadow of God on earth. All this was in startling contrast to the early original view of the caliph as the successor to the Prophet's temporal functions only, a first among equals obliged to consult with the community in what was essentially "mutual" consultation. Thus it seemed quite in order for the later type of caliph (and his judiciary) to judge infringements of the exclusive rights of God and of the ʿibādāt. Indeed, later legal works from about the tenth century of the Common Era define the rights of God as those of the state and society, and the rights of mankind as the private rights of an individual or a small group. The changed definition worked in reverse as well, so that almost any measure promulgated by the state easily slipped into being regarded as a right of (or duty towards) God.

In an ultimate sense, a value involves rights and duties toward God whether it is personal or social in significance; but the distinction between values that concern purely the rights of God and those that concern the rights of human beings as well acquires immediate importance when human beings endeavor to arrange their mutual affairs by consultation amongst themselves, as enjoined by the Qurʾān. By placing the state and the community in the perilously exalted position of representing God on earth in all matters and thus being theoretically empowered to punish all infringements of God's rights (even if powerless to reward obedience to them), classical thought was obliged to regard every act as being capable of compliance at the hands of the state, irrespective of whether the acts were so personal that only the All-Knowing God could accurately and effectively mete out justice, or were, on the contrary, those acts on which the state could properly and genuinely take action. The scale of values set out in the Qurʾān, originally and basically moral in quality, became increasingly overwhelmed by a legal scale applied to acts for which the law was not, and could not, be designed. Instead of the ethical values of Islam controlling the law, the legal system submerged the ethical values in the attempt to make every value conform to a legally enforceable rule.

The effect of this change became apparent in the pattern of the Five Values. When something was obligatory or forbidden, even if it concerned a pure right of (or duty towards) God, the law was obliged to assign a punishment, enforceable in this world, for any infraction instead of trusting in God to administer punishment, whether in this world or in the Hereafter.

Thus a denial of faith on the part of a Muslim for which no punishment to be administered by man is prescribed in the Qurʾān, where the matter is stated to be between God and the wrongdoer alone, became an offense for which the punishment was death for a Muslim man, and for a Muslim woman imprisonment for life or until she repented. Similarly with prayer, another right of (or duty towards) God, in classical Hanafi law the punishment for neglect was imprisonment, while the classical Maliki and Shafiʿi view was that the violator be asked to repent; if he failed to do so he was to be put to death.

The marked contrasts between the early and classical views and the damage done in later times to ethical sensitivity and respect for the effectiveness of the law provide one of the most important reasons for the desirability—indeed, the pressing necessity—of reopening the gate of *ijtihād,* that is, to reassert the right of directly understanding the Qurʾān and sunna in terms of their legal imperatives, rather than a blind imitation (*taqlīd*) of the verdicts of the late classical period. Without such ijtihād in actual practice, and not just in theory or mere lip service, current Islamic resurgence and its essential concomitant of a proper, consistent, authentic, and workable application of Islamic law cannot succeed.

These contrasts also raise in yet another form the difference between those who conceive of Islamic resurgence as requiring primary inspiration and guidance from the Qurʾān and sunna directly and from the early age of Islamic history, on the one hand, and those who seem to think that Islamic resurgence means nothing more than the resumption of Muslim theory and practice as it was when the postclassical era was abruptly broken by Western and Russian intrusions and conquests, on the other hand. The latter group do not admit any need for self-examination. They explain Muslim reverses as being due to the "treacherous conduct" of enemies, or such things as outside machinations and intrigues, and are unwilling to admit, let alone examine, the internal causes for the Muslim decline.

A reassertion of the spirit and practice of the early period implies, of course, the application of *sharīʿa,* but in terms relevant for today's time-space dimensions for which authority can be found in the famous ḥadīth concerning the appointment by the Prophet Muḥammad (o.w.b.p.) of Muʾādh b. Jabal as governor of Yemen,[6] and by the legislative activity of

[6]Reported in ḥadīth collections of Abū Daʾūd (d. 273/888) and al-Tirmidhī (d. 279/892) as follows: "The Prophet of Allāh asked, 'How will you decide when a matter comes to you for decision?' He replied, 'I shall decide according to the Book of Allāh.' He asked, 'If you do not find it in the Book of Allāh?' He replied, 'Then according to the sunna of the Messenger of Allāh.' He asked, 'If you do not find it in the sunna of the Messenger of Allāh?' He replied, 'Then I shall exert hard according to my opinion (*ijtihād ar-raʾy*) and spare no pains.' He narrated that the Prophet patted his chest and said, 'All praise is for Allāh who supplied the messenger of the Messenger of Allāh with what the Messenger of Allāh is pleased with.' "

such persons as ʿUmar b. al-Khaṭṭāb, the second caliph, in such matters as divorce.[7] For the Five Values the legal implications are to recognize that matters pertaining to God's rights can be rewarded or punished by Him Alone, and He may choose to do so in this world, or in the Hereafter, or in a combination of both.

It is only with respect to social transactions and criminal law that the state or society can rightfully seek to punish infringements or indicate the individual or group of individuals who are entitled to seek redress. Those rights are liable to be enforced by God, by punishment if He chooses at any time; and certainly only He can reward their faithful observance.

Only when this state of affairs is achieved once more can the human conscience be brought into effective play in the making of the good individual and thereby create a genuinely better society, composed as it must be of better individuals. The question arises at this point as to how this condition can be brought about. Legal reform requires an acceptable, workable institutional framework for the exercise of basic ijtihād once more, but the question of the Five Values involves ethics as much as it does law.[8]

Some may hold that changes in law can be effective only when there has been a prior change in ethical attitudes. Others may hold that the reverse is more valid, namely, that inculcating a particular ethical outlook can only be brought about after a prior change in law. Perhaps the process must be regarded as mutual and interdependent, with ethics and law developing hand in hand. Yet if a priority can be given it may be identified by resorting to the equally important need for change and reform in education, because only a healthy outlook in broad perspective can bring about healthy changes in particular matters. In Muslim terms this means that an overall, conformable Islamic ethical outlook has to be understood from the Qurʾān and from the Prophet's sunna before one can begin to comprehend the Islamic imperative on an individual matter. This, as I understand it, has been a major objective of Fazlur Rahman in his important book, *Major Themes of the Qurʾān.*[9]

Whether we consider education in terms of the mass media or of the school and university system, both traditional and contemporary, the teaching of Islamic ethics must stress the proper distinction between each of the Five Values. Thus, what is "disliked" should not be made "forbidden" or what is "recommended" should not be made "obligatory" because of the inability of state or society to reward as it can punish. Nor should there be any

[7]The second caliph made binding the *ṭalāq al-bidʿa* (the innovatory divorce) in which the triple pronouncement of divorce is made at one sitting without any time lapse between the three pronouncements.

[8]The legal institutional requirements are considered in Kemal A. Faruki, *Islamic Jurisprudence* (2d ed.; Karachi: National Book Foundation, 1975), pp. 152–165 and 187–224.

[9](Minneapolis: Bibliotheca Islamica, 1980).

confusion between God's rights (ḥuqūq Allāh) and the rights of mankind (ḥuqūq al-insān). This alone can cure the adulteration of the Five Values which had developed by classical times when the state or society attempted to stand in God's place in the writings of the jurists and in the courts.

If from an early educational stage a Muslim child is made aware of Islam's ethical precepts and outlook and of the reality of God's power with regard to their observance and nonobservance, if this awareness is fostered in the innermost recesses of the conscience, then, as such a child grows into a citizen of the state he or she will be far better able to understand and apply the socially enforceable aspects of Islamic rules.

The health of an Islamic society requires, above all, that a sense of *taqwā* permeate the individuals of which it is composed. Taqwā is an ever-growing awareness of God's total and continuous presence, everywhere and at all times, so that an individual's every act or omission is made with this increasingly acute awareness that God is present, anxious to reward but prepared to punish when and as He sees fit. The very opening verse of the first main chapter of the Qur'ān (al-Baqara) stresses that the Qur'ān is a guide only to those who possess taqwā—such are the importance and priority attached to a sensitive and awakened conscience.

This indeed is, possibly, the main purpose of the Islamic message here on earth: to help bring about in ever-increasing measure the role of conscience in the ethical and legal regulation of men's lives, whether collectively or singly, and to do so not merely outwardly but also inwardly, when only the Most Merciful and Just God and the individual concerned know of the thought and even the act.

# DIVINE JUSTICE AND HUMAN REASON IN MUᶜTAZILITE ETHICAL THEOLOGY

GEORGE F. HOURANI
State University of New York at Buffalo

## I

The Muᶜtazilite school of theology had a theoretical system of ethics, which was developed in a rather consistent fashion from the beginning of the school in the middle of the eighth century A.D. through the two Basran masters Jubbāʾī (d. 915) and Abū Hāshim (d. 933) to its culmination in the great *Mughnī* of qadi ᶜAbd al-Jabbār (d. 1025).[1] The theory is well known in its main lines and has been set forth systematically and in detail in my book *Islamic Rationalism: the Ethics of ᶜAbd al-Jabbār.*[2] I shall not go over that ground again here, but shall offer some reflections on the system under certain headings, with the intention to bring out its character and historical fate and to estimate briefly its merits as a theory of ethics. The system will be discussed within the context of Sunnite Islam, where it was formed, although later on its influence survived better in the Shiᶜite milieu.

## II

We can find in Muᶜtazilite ethics a sincere ethical purpose, which the school pursued in an honest manner within the bounds of what they thought could be demonstrated as true. This purpose may be summed up as the vindication and encouragement of a measure of freedom and power to act in human beings, as against the crushing weight of divine omnipotence as it was interpreted by Traditionalists. The Muᶜtazilite ideal was supported by a few convictions that the Muᶜtazilites attempted to demonstrate and elaborate, which may be summed up under the following headings:

[1] *al-Mughnī fī abwāb at-tawḥīdi wa l-ᶜadl,* various editors (Cairo, 1962–70). See especially part VI, vol. i, ed. A. F. Ahwani and I. Madkour. Hereafter *M.*

[2] (Oxford, 1971). Hereafter *IR*.

(a) Ethical attributes such as "just," "obligatory," "good," and "evil" have a real, objective existence. They are applicable to the acts of both God and man.

(b) Human beings have power to act, independently of the divine will or material circumstances.

(c) Human beings also have the power to know objective ethical truths and make ethical judgments to some extent by direct thought or "reason" (*ʿaql*), not merely by interpreting scripture—a function in which the ulama are clearly superior and would therefore exercise final authority over the lives of lay persons.

## III

How did the Muʿtazilites arrive at their conclusions? Their method of research was essentially theological, a method of kalam as understood in Islam, being based on their interpretation of scripture, the Qurʾān. This interpretation is selective, choosing certain teachings of the Qurʾān as fundamental. The primary principle emphasized by the Muʿtazilites was the justice of God—one of the two principles according to which they called themselves "the party of justice and unity."

Taking off from this principle, the Muʿtazilites did not quote the Qurʾān at every turn, as their opponents did, but rather made extensive inferences from the principle of justice, working out an entire system of what it implies for the nature and acts of God, His relations with man, and man's ethical life. They developed this system under the stimulus of debate among themselves and with Muslim opponents, in the course of which they employed some linguistic and some empirical arguments. This means that their method was to a limited extent philosophical, in a modern sense, although they did not recognize it as such.

The method of exposition was generally dialectical, consisting of objections and answers in the formula "If they say . . . it is said to them. . . ." This was the characteristic method of kalam. ʿAbd al-Jabbār opens each chapter with a short statement of his position, then proceeds to an interminable series of objections and answers, often confusing in its complexity.

## IV

The core of this paper consists of a sketch of the logic of the Muʿtazilite system of ethics. By displaying such a logical system I hope to make intelligible the cohesion and consistency of the school in the sphere of theological ethics over a period of three centuries. I shall state three premises, then some conclusions drawn from them.

(a) The starting point is an ontological premise about the nature of ethical value: that terms such as "just," "obligatory," and "evil" refer to objective facts of the world in any particular context. This position is held in conscious opposition to that of the Traditionalists (the jurists, Hanbalites, Ashᶜarites, Zahirites), that any ethical term applied to human acts, thoughts, or desires means nothing but "commanded," "permitted," or "forbidden by God." The principle of the objectivity of value is much insisted on, because it is the primary foundation of the rest of the theory. The Muᶜtazilites of Baṣra worked out their definitions of these objective meanings in terms of what deserves to be approved, tolerated, or disapproved. For example, "An obligatory act is one for whose omission the agent deserves blame," "An evil act is one for whose commission the agent deserves blame" (*IR,* 39). The definitions do not refer to what *is* blamed by God or man, because in that case they would be subjective, referring to someone's actual attitudes towards the object valued; and that would lead straight into the error of the Traditionalists. (Why their view was an error will be explained later.)[3]

(b) The next step is a theological premise: that God is completely just in the sense defined. This premise is supported strongly by the usage of "just" in the Qurʾān as applicable to God, while the Traditionalist definition as "commanded by God" makes no sense in reference to His justice. At this point ᶜAbd al-Jabbār draws a fine line. He admits that it is logically possible (*mumkin*) for God to be unjust, but it is inadmissible (*lā yajūz*) that He would in fact be so (*IR,* 97–102). It is inadmissible on both rational and moral grounds. But we need not go further into the details of the arguments. The distinction was drawn to preserve divine omnipotence.

Some earlier Muᶜtazilites, however, Naẓẓām, Aswārī, and Jāḥiẓ, went to the more logical extreme of saying that God in His nature as the perfect being could not be unjust without self-contradiction; and, as everyone admitted, self-contradiction is impossible even for God, and that does not count as a real limitation on His omnipotence.

(c) Another theological premise concerns God's relations with man: that He will reward the just and punish the unjust in a life after death. This was a major doctrine of the Qurʾān, repeated over and again and accepted by all Muslims.

Several conclusions were drawn from these premises.

(i) If God is to be just in His rewarding and punishing, He must give men a fair chance to be just or unjust on their own responsibility. This principle is supported not only as a consequence of the preceding premises but by implication in the Qurʾān, which states several times that God does not

[3] The Muᶜtazilite definitions are the same as those proposed by A. C. Ewing in *The Definition of Good* (New York, 1947), ch. 5: "Good" means "fitting object of a pro attitude," "bad" means "fitting object of an anti attitude."

impose on anyone duties beyond his power. The fact that the principle contradicts predestination, which is also apparently supported by the Qurʾān, was taken by the Muʿtazilites as a reason why the Qurʾān must be interpreted in a way that denies predestination. Much effort was expended by them in solving this problem of interpretation.

Regardless of theological interpretations, the principle of human responsibility had to be accepted by Muslim jurists for practical reasons. It was enshrined as an axiom of shariʿa law: "Capacity is a condition of obligation" (*al-istiṭāʿa sharṭ at-taklīf*). It is also well known to Western ethical philosophers as the dictum of Immanuel Kant: "'Ought' implies 'can.'" But in Islam, with its belief in everlasting punishment for evildoers, the principle had to be taken even more seriously. Hence even predestinarian theologians such as Ashʿarī made the utmost effort to reconcile their dogma with human responsibility, through the ingenious doctrine that man "acquires" (*yaktasib*) his own acts and thus in some way becomes responsible for them.

This power to act implies, in the Muʿtazilite view, power to choose freely between different possible acts. Therefore man must have free choice. Such a view is supported not only by deduction from the previous arguments but also by the common sense of mankind.

God alone is the ultimate source of all power: "There is no power and no strength except in God!" (*lā hawla wa lā quwwa illā billāh!*), in the frequently used exclamation. But God has delegated to man power over his own acts, within the limits set by the forces of nature. Thus man is responsible for his own fate, which will be deserved according to divine justice. So he is rescued from the injustice of predestination, as expressed eloquently in the familiar words of Edward Fitzgerald's translation of a quatrain (*rubʿiyya*) by ʿUmar Khayyām:

> O Thou, who didst with pitfall and with gin
> Beset the path I was to wander in,
> Thou would'st not with predestination round
> Beset me, and impute my fall to sin!

The Muʿtazilites saw another merit in their doctrine of divine delegation of power to man. Since many human acts are evil, God is not the cause of this kind of evil in the world. Consequently a large part of the problem of theodicy is solved.

(ii) If man is to be able by his own delegated power to live rightly and deserve to receive reward and avoid punishment, he must be able to know what is right and what is wrong. The Muʿtazilite theory of ethical knowledge is elaborated in the *Mughnī* (*IR*, ch. 2).[4]

[4] See also M. Bernand, *Le Problème de la connaissance d'après le Mugnī du cadi ʿAbd al-Gabbār* (Algiers, 1982).

Since "justice," "obligation," "evil," and the other ethical terms have objective meanings, man has direct intellectual access to a knowledge of how these meanings can be predicated truly both of particular acts and thoughts and of general rules of conduct. Thus anyone can know the main obligations and prohibitions of life by his "reason" (ᶜaql), which includes the use of empirical observations and inferences:

> Know that the will for evil is necessarily evil, because whoever knows it to be such a will know its evil character, and that its agent deserves blame, just as whoever knows that wrongdoing is wrong knows its evil character. (*M,* VI.i.62)

Another example:

> It is known immediately that a lie, carrying no benefit and no repulsion of injury greater than it, and an injury carrying no benefit greater than it, which is not deserved or thought to be deserved, when a free and capable person performs them, are both deserving of blame, if there is no overriding consideration [lit. if there is nothing to prevent that]. (*M,* VI.i.18)

We notice how carefully the qadi hedges the last statement, with a reference to the intention of the agent and a statement of the doctrine of prima facie right and wrong, as worked out in modern times by the British rationalist David Ross.[5]

This doctrine of rational ethical knowledge had attractive features for Muslims and non-Muslims. It could rescue ordinary Muslims, including rulers, from the domination of shariᶜa lawyers as experts in ethical decisions claiming to give binding interpretations of scriptural texts. And it would give a chance for salvation to non-Muslims, such as pre-Islamic peoples.

Can we know all our obligations by natural reason? No; natural reason has to be supplemented by revelation on details, such as the value of prayer and the specific manner of performing it (*IR,* 33–34, 135). Moreover, revelation had a second important function, to motivate right conduct and thought by its teaching of promise and threat.

These considerations went some way towards answering the objection of Traditionalists that rationalism made revelation useless. The Muᶜtazilites also accepted to some extent the Qurᵓān's insistence that man left to himself follows his selfish desires and does not know what is right; he is very much in need of guidance by revelation.

(iii) The value of revelation provided another argument against predestination. If God had necessitated that believers would believe and unbelievers

[5] David Ross, *The Right and the Good* (Oxford, 1930).

would not, these acts would occur from them with or without the stimulation of the Book and prophets. "But every doctrine that implies the uselessness of scriptures and messengers must be false" (*M,* VI.ii, 348–49), (*IR,* 136–37).

(iv) The justice of God demands that He could not lie or mislead men in His revelations to them. For that would deliberately lead believers in scripture to sin and be punished for their sins. Such an act on His part would be a wicked portrayal of their faith in His truthfulness, and is inadmissible as an act of a good God (*IR,* 102, 130–31).

## V

The Muʿtazilite ethical theory was developed in the course of prolonged dialogues among themselves and against Traditionalists. As usual, such dialogues led to a strengthening of defenses on both sides. We must look at some of the objections in both directions.

On the Muʿtazilite side, at its culmination in the last two decades of the tenth century when the *Mughnī* was written, we can see ʿAbd al-Jabbār considering exhaustively every possible objection and going over to the offensive against the opponents. Here I shall consider only the latter side of his dialectic, some of his refutations of ethical voluntarism, the Traditionalist theory.

(i) The character of an act of being obligatory is different from being commanded. To command is to indicate that someone wants something done: "It does not imply the obligatoriness of what is commanded" (*M,* XVII.113). There are commands without obligation and obligations that are not commanded (*IR,* 56–58).

(ii) If "evil" meant nothing but "forbidden," an act forbidden by a human being, such as a caliph or sultan, should have a certain force in making the act evil. But it does not, because human prohibitions do not altogether correspond with the evil character of acts. Also, human prohibitions may contradict divine prohibitions.

This type of argument is weak, because Traditionalists specified "commanded or prohibited by God" as the defining characteristics of obligatory and evil acts, respectively (*IR,* 58–59).

(iii) If God were to do wrong or command us to tell lies, these acts would still be recognizable by us as evil, and that fact would again show up the difference between being good and being His acts or commands (*IR,* 59–60).

The Traditionalists were challenged to assert that lying, for instance, would indeed be good if God were to perform it or command us to do so. Some Traditionalists, such as Ashʿarī and Ibn Ḥazm, accepted this consequence without blinking an eye, but added that God in His mercy had never lied or issued a command to man to do so; in fact, the Qurʿān is constantly condemning lying and those who called the Prophet a liar. So the possibility that God might command us to be liars is remote and not something we need to worry about.

(iv) If command by God were the essence of obligation, pre-Islamic people, Hindus, and materialists would not know their obligations. But they do know them: "—any sane person knows his obligations even though he does not know that—there is a commander and forbidder" (*M,* VI.i.45), (*IR,* 60).

The Qurʾān in fact implies in many statements that knowledge of what is obligatory, good, and evil is accessible to everyone:

> Surely God bids to justice and good-doing and giving to kinsmen, and He forbids indecency, dishonor and insolence. (XVI.92)

These virtues and vices must have been understood as such prior to the coming of revelation.

(v) The Traditionalists claimed that no acts of God could be evil because God is not under any higher Lord who might forbid them. But in that case the corresponding rule would have to apply to His supposed good acts: They could not be good because they are not commanded by a superior being.

(vi) Finally, ᶜAbd al-Jabbār explains how "forbidden by God" came to be considered equivalent to "evil": It occurred because God was seen to forbid only evil things. But He forbids them *because* they are evil—an independent concept, prior to His forbidding.

## VI

### Traditionalist refutations of Muᶜtazilite ethics

(i) The definitions of ethical words such as "right" in terms of "deserving blame, praise," and so on, were criticized on the ground that they introduce another value word into the definiens, namely, "deserving." This word means "right to be blamed, blameworthy," so that the definition is circular. ᶜAbd al-Jabbār attempts to answer the objection by explaining that there is an objective, fitting relation between the agent of an act and the judgment passed on him. Still, the qadi could be pressed further by an opponent who would point out that "fitting," too, is a value term, meaning the same as "right" or "just" (*IR,* 44–47).[6]

It is possible to avoid this difficulty by adopting Aristotle's concept of justice as equality, modified in various ways. Equality is a mathematical concept, and although it cannot be applied in a rigorous way to human affairs, as Aristotle realized well, it remains a concept which does not itself

[6] For similar criticisms of Ewing's definition of "good" see R. B. Brandt, "Blameworthiness and Obligation," in Abraham I. Melden, ed., *Essays in Moral Philosophy* (Seattle, 1958), pp. 3–39, and O. A. Johnson, *Rightness and Goodness* (The Hague, 1959), pp. 153–155.

have value embedded in it; yet it is the ultimate basis of the definitions of "just," "fitting," and "deserving," which are value concepts. This is not the place to argue such a theory of justice. In any case, the Muʿtazilites did not follow this line of reasoning, as far as I know. In consequence, Traditionalists could claim a victory over them at this crucial point. Since no true objective definitions of value words had been found, Traditionalism held the field with its simpler (and apparently more religious) definitions of these words in terms of commands and prohibitions of God.

A parallel may be seen in the history of modern Anglo-Saxon ethical philosophy. The Utilitarianism of J. Bentham and J. S. Mill gained wide acceptance in the nineteenth century, with its definition of the good in its social meaning as "the greatest happiness of the greatest number." Weak points in the theory were pointed out by several philosophers in the early twentieth century—G. E. Moore, H. Rashdall, H. A. Pritchard, D. Ross, and others—who adopted various forms of rationalism, generally grouped together as Intuitionism. But these theories had their own difficulty in the sphere of epistemology: How does one "intuit" ethical truths, and if the process is meant to lead to certainty, how does it happen that there are apparently irresolvable differences of opinion on ethical issues between intelligent persons?

Such criticisms of all kinds of objectivism, both naturalistic and intuitionist, as well as of descriptive subjectivism, led a number of philosophers in the mid-twentieth century to abandon in despair all types of descriptive definitions of ethical terms and resort to prescriptive theories of the use of ethical terms, such as those of C. Stevenson and R. M. Hare. Such a view has gained wide popularity, even to the extent of becoming a kind of orthodoxy in intellectual circles. It has a common feature with Islamic Traditionalism in reducing ethical language to a system of commands or prescriptions. This position is also closely related to positive theories of law.

But how much more powerful in its appeal is Traditionalist Islam, as compared with modern prescriptivism or legal positivism, in being able to refer ethical value to the commands and prohibitions of almighty God through revelation, not merely to any human will! It may not have occurred to modern prescriptivists that they are playing right into the hands of religious fundamentalism, which is enjoying a revival in Christian and Jewish as well as Muslim nations.

Contrary to the actual outcome of this debate between Muʿtazilites and Traditionalists, the Muʿtazilite ontology of value should have won the debate on intellectual grounds accepted by both parties, because the objectivity of ethical value is asserted or implied all through the Qurʾān. In a recent article in *The Muslim World,*[7] I have shown conclusively the absurdity of

[7] "Ethical Presuppositions of the Qurʾān," *The Muslim World,* 70 (1980), 1–28.

voluntarist interpretations at many points in the scripture of Islam. For instance, the repeated commands of God to do what is right would be empty of force and insipid if they meant only "commands to do what He commands." It is even harder to make sense of statements that God is always just to His servants on the supposition that "just" means "commanded by God." The only possible move at this point is to resort to the transcendence of meaning in reference to God—always the last refuge of baffled theologians. In the present case it deprives "justice" of any meaning intelligible to human beings.

(ii) The Muʿtazilite theory of ethical knowledge was vulnerable in its claim that reason gives certain knowledge of many principles of ethics. This claim was challenged directly by showing disagreements in opinions, which could not occur if the disagreeing parties had both true rational intuitions and the same knowledge of the facts.[8]

(iii) The theory allows to scripture only a supplementary role, a position which contradicts the Qurʾān's heavy emphasis on revelation as the only sure guide to right living. According to the Qurʾān, man left to himself follows his fancies and personal desires, which lead him into selfish, immoral ways of life.

## VII

In spite of its great intellectual strength, the Muʿtazilite theory of ethics was defeated in the public forum of history, at any rate in the Sunnite countries, which eventually comprised the majority of Muslims in the world. The defeat occurred by suppression, not so much in their earlier crisis when the caliph Mutawakkil (847–861) turned against them, but more decisively through decrees of the caliph Qādir in 1017 and 1041.

We must inquire into the reasons for this final setback. The obvious explanation is that Muʿtazilite ethics were rejected by most of the ulama as part of a wider rejection of other doctrines, such as the creation of the Qurʾān, to which the Traditionalists objected even more strongly. There was, however, a deeper objection to the entire rationalist method of inquiry into questions of law and ethics. The whole class of ulama, including the Muʿtazilites, had their basic education in Islamic law and jurisprudence, including long years spent in memorizing the Qurʾān and *ḥadīth*. In this field the question of method and sources had already been settled decisively by the theoretical studies of Shāfiʿī (767–820) in favor of a positive law, to be derived as far as possible from texts, their extension through analogies, and their supplementation by consensus. Except in Muʿtazilite circles, this

[8]See G. F. Hourani, "Juwaynī's Criticisms of Muʿtazilite Ethics," *The Muslim World,* 65 (1975), 161–173, especially 164–168.

attitude was carried over to questions which we now consider ethical but not legal, but which were then considered to be within the sphere of divine law, the shariʿa. Compared with the exercise of rational *ijtihād* demanded by the Muʿtazilites, how much easier and safer to refer all such questions to positive sources, which could be looked up, at first in the original sources, later in the copious books of the four great imams of Sunnite law, such as the *Muwaṭṭāʾ* of Mālik, and later still in shorter compendia like Qayrawānī's *Risāla.*

Hostility to the Muʿtazilite movement was shown both by Traditionalist theologians of the school of Ashʿarī and by the antitheology Hanbalites. Both groups by the eleventh century were well organized, and the latter could draw on popular support for protests and demonstrations. The Muʿtazilites were individuals with few supporters in eleventh-century Baghdad. Thus it was possible for Ashʿarites and Hanbalites to exert pressure on the caliph Qādir to issue his decrees demanding a Traditionalist profession of faith and renunciation of Muʿtazilite opinions and public teaching. These decrees did not arise from any firm theological convictions of the caliph, but solely from a desire to placate the majority of the Sunnite ulama. He evidently perceived it as their common interest to present a solid front against the Shiʿite Buwayhid sultans who were the temporal rulers of Iraq.

Thus the fall of the Muʿtazilite movement was due to political repression, and it occurred even before the Seljūq sultans occupied Baghdad in 1055 and initiated a policy of founding madrasas to train Shafiʿite lawyers and Ashʿarite theologians.[9]

## VIII

In considering the effects of the defeat of ethical objectivism and rationalism (in a broad sense), we must take account not just of a few professional Muʿtazilites, but also of philosophers and scientists who held the same view of ethics, in line with the main Greek tradition; of Hanafite lawyers who were often sympathetic to the Muʿtazilite movement and had long been using their independent judgments on legal and ethical questions; and of a much larger educated public who had been inarticulately following these leaders of opinion. If we bear all this in mind we can see that the newly enforced Traditionalist orthodoxy must have had a serious effect in weakening confident moral convictions among the educated Muslim public, except for those ulama who because of their expertise in interpreting the shariʿa now became the official arbiters of ethical questions.

[9] For the narration and background of these events see G. Makdisi's monumental study, *Ibn ʿAqīl et la résurgence de l'Islām traditionaliste au XIe siècle (Ve siècle de l'Hégire)* (Damascus, 1963), ch. 4.

The only force that could stand against them was that of sultans, who continued to exercise their own judgments, sometimes on ethical grounds, sometimes in their own interests. But sultans usually did not need to defy the scholars, because they could generally obtain from them an appropriate *fatwā* to support any decision. Thus the Ottoman sultans built up a network of *qānūns* or state laws with the official approval of their muftis.

As a consequence of this and other factors, the intellectual environment from the eleventh to the nineteenth century was unfavorable to the moral, political, and economic reforms demanded by justice in Muslim countries because there was no public available to lead and support them on their own merits. The only possible path to change was through religious revival movements led by a Mahdi or a Sufi, and these usually ended in one more hereditary autocracy no better than its predecessors. I believe that the decline of the Muᶜtazilite movement, with its conviction of an objective justice intelligible directly by the human mind, was one of the events that weakened Islamic civilization for some eight centuries.

## IX

The great merit of the Muᶜtazilite theory in the Islamic context was that it encouraged independent thinking on ethical questions by laymen and "clergy" (the ulama). Further, as I have shown in my article "Ethical presuppositions of the Qurʾān,"[10] objectivism is the basic belief of the Qurʾān itself, so that the Muᶜtazilite had the strongest Islamic authority for their first premise.

As a modern theory also, although it shares a weakness with A. C. Ewing's Intuitionism, discussed above in VI (i), the Muᶜtazilite theory contains the nucleus of an objective, naturalistic theory, if we take into account that "reason" (ᶜaql) covers a wide range of mental processes, including consideration in ethical judgment of benefits as well as justice. These are the two elements of the social meaning of the good, whose combination I believe constitutes the strongest formula yet reached in modern ethical philosophy. I hope that Muslim philosophers and theologians will revive and revise the Muᶜtazilite theory in modern terms.

[10] See n. 7.

# NAṢĪR AD-DĪN ṬŪSĪ'S ETHICS BETWEEN PHILOSOPHY, SHIᶜISM, AND SUFISM

WILFERD MADELUNG
Oxford University

Naṣīr ad-Dīn Ṭūsī completed his *Nasirean Ethics* (*Akhlāq-e Nāṣerī*), the most highly esteemed book on ethics in Persian, around the year 633/1235 while in the service of the Ismāᶜīlī governor of Qohestān, the Muḥtasham Naṣīr ad-Dīn ᶜAbd ar-Raḥīm b. Abī Manṣūr. He named the work after his learned patron, who had commissioned him to write it, and opened it with a dedication to him in the flowery style of the time in which he also invoked the blessings of the contemporary Ismāᶜīlī imam, ᶜAlāᵓ ad-Dīn Muḥammad.[1] Two decades later Ṭūsī parted company with the Ismāᶜīlīs, whose power was broken by the Mongol conquest and the surrender of ᶜAlāᵓ ad-Dīn's son and successor, Khūrshāh, in 654/1256. He then replaced the laudatory dedication of the book with a new preamble containing a Sunni formula of benediction for the Prophet Muḥammad, his Family, and his Companions. Ṭūsī went on to explain that his stay with the Ismāᶜīlīs in Qohestān had been involuntary and that his eulogy of their leaders was motivated by the necessity of self-preservation. The book itself, however, dealt with one of the disciplines of philosophy and as such was unrelated to any religious school or community. Students of different creeds had therefore eagerly perused it, so that numerous manuscripts of it were circulated among men. Thus he felt obliged to replace the original dedication and to publish the truth of the matter in the hope that future copyists would spread the book in its new form.[2]

The *Nasirean Ethics* clearly belongs, as suggested by Ṭūsī here, to the tradition of Islamic philosophy rooted in Greek and Hellenistic thought. Ṭūsī himself summarily acknowledged some of his main sources. His patron, the Muḥtasham, had initially proposed that Ṭūsī translate Miskawayh's well-known ethical compendium *Tahdhīb al-akhlāq* from the Arabic into

[1] Jalāl ad-Dīn Homāᵓi, *Moqaddama-ye qadīm-e Akhlāq-e Nāṣerī* (Tehran, 1335/1958), pp. 9–15.

[2] *Akhlāq-e Nāṣerī,* ed. M. Mīnovī and ᶜA. Ḥaidarī (Tehran, 1356/1979), pp. 33–35.

Persian. After some consideration Ṭūsī decided against this in the belief that he would be unable to convey fully the polished elegance of the original. He also was aware of a need for a comprehensive book on practical philosophy comprising its three branches: ethics, economics, and politics, while Miskawayh had dealt with only the first of these. Ṭūsī therefore undertook to write a new work whose first section, on ethics, would be broadly based on the *Tahdhīb al-akhlāq.*[3] His primary source in the section on economics was, as he later states,[4] a treatise on the subject by Avicenna, which has been identified as the *Kitāb as-Siyāsa.* He also used, it has been shown, the Arabic translation of the *Oikonomikos* of the Greek Bryson,[5] which he mentions in passing. The section on politics was based, according to Ṭūsī, on "the sayings and aphorisms (*aqvāl o nokat*)" of al-Fārābī.[6] More specifically, al-Fārābī's *as-Siyāsa al-madaniyya,* his *Fuṣūl al-madanī,* and his admonitions quoted in Miskawayh's *al-Ḥikma al-khālida* can clearly be recognized as sources for the *Nasirean Ethics,* though Ṭūsī also seems to have had at his disposal one or more treatises by al-Fārābī which have not yet been identified.[7]

It must be stressed that Ṭūsī used these sources loosely and with considerable freedom. Literal translation varies with paraphrase and independent elaboration. His presentation, if not his subject matter, is often original and fuller than in his sources. The traditional philosophical scope and frame, however, are apparently not infringed by this liberty. Ṭūsī gives assurance of his personal detachment by stressing at the end of the introduction:

> Let me say that what is recorded in this book, covering all aspects of Practical Philosophy (whether by way of relation or anecdote, or in the form of chronicles or narrative), is repeated from ancient and modern philosophers; not even a beginning is made to confirm the true or disprove the false, nor—in respect to our own convictions—do we

[3] Ibid., p. 36.

[4] Ibid., p. 208.

[5] See M. Plessner, *Der "Oikonomikos" des Neupythagoräers Bryson und sein Einfluss auf die islamische Wissenschaft* (Heidelberg, 1928), pp. 52–55. Plessner suggests (p. 42) that there may have been a more extensive version of Avicenna's *Kitāb as-siyāsa* than the one edited by L. Maʿlūf in *Mashriq,* 9 (1906).

[6] *Akhlāq-e Nāṣerī,* p. 248.

[7] For detailed identification of Ṭūsī's sources see especially M. T. Dāneshpazhūh in the introduction to his edition of Ṭūsī's *Akhlāq-e Moḥtashamī* (Tehran, 1339/1962), pp. 19–23, and the annotation by the editors to *Akhlāq-e Nāṣerī.* Dāneshpazhūh's suggestion that al-Fārābīs *Ārāʾ ahl al-madīna al-fāḍila* is a source of Sections 1, 3, and 4 of the Third Discourse seems incorrect. The same work is also named as a source of Ṭūsī's by E. I. J. Rosenthal, *Political Thought in Medieval Islam* (Cambridge, 1958), p. 212, and the editors of *Akhlāq-e Nāṣerī* (p. 388). No positive evidence, however, has been given. The section beginning p. 289, l. 10, is based on *as-Siyāsa al-madaniyya,* rather than *Ārāʾ ahl al-madīna al-fāḍila,* as the editors suggest (p. 395).

> engage to support any opinion or to condemn any particular school of thought. Thus, if the reader encounters an ambiguity on a point, or regards any question as open to objection, he should recognize that the author of this book has no responsibility for rejoinder, and offers no surety for uncovering the face of accuracy.[8]

The book was thus addressed to all scholars, students, and dilettantes of philosophy irrespective of their religious beliefs. They were encouraged to read it as a digest of traditional practical philosophy without worrying about the personal engagement and views of the author and his Ismāʿīlī patrons. As Ṭūsī suggests in his later preamble, many of his contemporaries had read and come to appreciate the book as just such a digest. Most later readers have no doubt also viewed it in this perspective.

Yet does this perspective exhaustively comprehend the motivation of the *Nasirean Ethics*? The problem may be approached through a further question. Was Ṭūsī entirely sincere in affirming, in his later preamble, that philosophy was equally unrelated to all religious schools and communities? Philosophy of Greek origin was in the age of Ṭūsī overwhelmingly repudiated as incompatible with Islam by the guardians of orthodoxy, Sunni and Twelver Shiʿi alike. There had been and still were, to be sure, Sunni and Twelver Shiʿi philosophers who held that Islam was not incompatible with philosophy. They generally did not mix philosophy and religion, however, but viewed philosophy as a truth for the intellectual elite, while the same truth, on an intellectually less demanding level, was reflected in religion and in this form was more suitable for the common people. The attitude of the Ismāʿīlīs toward Greek philosophy was entirely different. A Neoplatonic cosmology lay at the very core of their esoteric religious teaching at least since its adoption and adaptation by the Transoxanian *dāʿī* (missionary) Muḥammad b. Aḥmad an-Nasafī in the early fourth/tenth century. A century later, the dāʿī Ḥamīd ad-Dīn al-Kirmānī had similarly adapted the cosmological concepts of al-Fārābī to Ismāʿīlī doctrine. Ismāʿīlīs thus had come to view philosophy as neither incompatible with their religion nor as a separate statement of the truth but as identical, at least in part. Of course, not all philosophical thought and opinions were acceptable to them. The Ismāʿīlī dāʿī and Persian poet Nạser-e Khosrau in his *Book combining the two Wisdoms* (*Kitāb jāmiʿ al-ḥikmatain*) discussed agreement and disagreement of the prophetic wisdom of Ismāʿīlī gnosis and philosophical wisdom. The heresiographer Tāj ad-Dīn ash-Shahrastānī, a secret Ismāʿīlī sympathizer, wrote a refutation of some principles of Avicenna's metaphysics from

[8] *Akhlāq-e Nāṣerī,* p. 43. The translation here and throughout follows the faithful and sensitive rendering of C. M. Wickens, *The Nasirean Ethics* (London, 1964), p. 31, with a few changes.

an Ismāʿīlī point of view, entitling it *The Wrestling Match* (*Kitāb al-Muṣāraʿa*).[9] It was to be, he explained, a daring philosophical wrestling match in which he engaged with the grand master of the Muslim philosophers on his own rational grounds. Yet it is evident that he entered into it with a philosophical platform not fully derived from his own reasoning. He himself admits to having drunk from the cup of prophetic revelation.

Ismāʿīlī philosophy was not meant to be a matter of free, unfettered rational investigation but a rational ascent under the guiding instruction (*taʿlīm*) of the infallible imam. The idea of the imam as the divinely guided, infallible teacher of mankind was vital in much of Shiʿi thought. Among the Ismāʿīlīs, Ḥasan-e Ṣabbāḥ, the founder of the Nizārī branch and first lord of Alamūt, had developed a sophisticated doctrine of taʿlīm demonstrating that human reason must inevitably go astray without the guiding instruction of the *muʿallim,* the infallible imam.[10] The Nizārīs were henceforth commonly known as the Taʿlīmīs, and al-Ghazālī in his refutation of Ismāʿīlīsm attacked primarily this doctrine as their central belief.

Ṭūsī himself wrote, no doubt after his dissociation from the Ismāʿīlīs, a refutation of ash-Shahrastānī's arguments against Avicenna in his *Wrestling Match* with the title *The Downfalls of the Wrestler* (*Maṣāriʿ al-muṣāriʿ*). In it he mercilessly ridiculed ash-Shahrastānī's pretense in challenging Avicenna, exposed the heretical Ismāʿīlī motivation of his arguments, and accused him of ignoring the most elementary notions of logic. Clearly ash-Shahrastānī's crypto-Ismāʿīlī ideology was in his eyes of no relevance to true philosophy. In the light of this devastating judgment there is no good reason to doubt the sincerity of Ṭūsī's assertion in his new preamble to the *Nasirean Ethics,* that philosophy was equally unrelated to all religious schools and communities. The so-called philosophy of the Ismāʿīlīs was a fake and their devotion to the pure truth a false pretense.

Yet Ṭūsī had not always thought so. In a spiritual autobiography[11] addressed to his Ismāʿīlī patrons, which he wrote some years after the *Nasirean Ethics,* he described the path that had led him to find his religious home among the Nizārī Taʿlīmīs, much as al-Ghazālī described his own path to spiritual peace among the Sufis in his famous *Deliverer from Error* (*al-Munqidh min aḍ-ḍalāl*). Ṭūsī had been brought up, he explains, among men who believed and followed only the exoteric aspect of the Law (*sharīʿa*)

[9] *K. Muṣāraʿat al-falāsifa,* ed. Suhayr Muḥammad Mukhtār (Cairo, 1976). For an analysis of the work and its refutation by Ṭūsī see W. Madelung, "Aš-Šahrastānīs Streitschrift gegen Avicenna und ihre Widerlegung durch Naṣīr ad-Dīn aṭ-Ṭūsī," in A. Dietrich, ed., *Akten des VII. Kongresses für Arabistik und Islamwissenschaft* (Göttingen, 1976), pp. 250–259.

[10] See especially M. G. S. Hodgson, *The Order of Assassins* (The Hague, 1955), pp. 51–58.

[11] First published under the title *Sair o solūk* by an anonymous editor in Tehran and republished by Modarres Reḍavī in *Majimūʿa-ye rasāʾel az taʾlīfāt-e . . . Khᵛāja Naṣīr ad-Dīn* (Tehran, 1335/1958), pp. 36–55.

and relatives whose only learning was in the exoteric sciences. From other sources it is known that they were Twelver Shiʿis. Ṭūsī himself, he goes on to explain, at first merely studied the roots and the branches of their school doctrine and thought that there could be nothing besides it. His father, however, who had seen the world and had been educated by his maternal uncle, a disciple of Tāj ad-Dīn ash-Shahrastānī, was less insistent on following these principles and rather encouraged him to study all kinds of sciences and listen to scholars of different schools and principles. Ṭūsī's specific mention of ash-Shahrastānī, whom he even calls the grand dāʿī (*dāʿī d-duʿāt*), suggests that the latter's crypto-Ismāʿīlī thought may have played an important role in his spiritual development though he does not further elaborate on it. He then became attached, on his father's recommendation, to a student of Afḍal ad-Dīn Kāshī, who taught him primarily mathematics. His teacher ever criticized the speech of the adherents of exoteric learning and pointed out the contradictions into which the followers of the letter of the sharīʿa inevitably fall. Yet whenever Ṭūsī tried to elicit more profound discourse from him, he declined reminding him of his youth and consoling him that he would find the truth later in his life if he kept seeking it. Ṭūsī next studied speculative theology (*kalām*) but soon discovered that it was entirely based on the letter of the sharīʿa and that its adherents employed their reason merely to defend their inherited creed. He then studied philosophy and found it highly rewarding since the students of this science gave their reason free rein in the search of the truth and did not confine it to following a certain convention. When the philosophical discourse reached its ultimate ends, however, namely the recognition of God and the knowledge of the Origin and Destination (of man), he found their principles shaky; for the intellect is unable to comprehend the Donor of the Intellect (*vāheb-e ʿaql*) and the First Principles (*mabādeʾ*). Since the philosophers in their conceit were misled to rely solely on their own speculation and reason, they stumbled in this field and talked on the basis of mere conjecture and wishful fancy. They employed reason in what was beyond its limits. Ṭūsī thus became aware of the need for taʿlīm, transcendent instruction, of a teacher who could guide the human intellect from potentiality to actuality, from deficiency to perfection. He then came by chance upon a copy of the *Sacred Articles* (*Foṣūl-e moqaddas*) of imam Ḥasan ʿalā dhikrihi s-salām, the proclaimer of the Resurrection in Alamūt in 559/1164. Ṭūsī's eyes were opened and he decided to join the Ismāʿīlīs.

It was thus as a philosopher and out of philosophical concerns that Ṭūsī converted to the Taʿlīmī faith. He did not give up his own philosophical faith but hoped to perfect and transcend it through the guidance of the infallible teacher. We may thus be encouraged to read the *Nasirean Ethics* from an Ismāʿīlī perspective and to search closely, in spite of Ṭūsī's assertion that all its contents were taken from the ancient and modern philosophers, for some hints as to where he may have seen their thought as specifically relevant to the Ismāʿīlī faith.[12]

Concerning practical philosophy, comprising ethics, economics, and politics, and its relationship to the law, Ṭūsī states:

> It should be recognized that the principles of beneficial works and virtuous acts on the part of the human species (implying the ordering of their affairs and states) lie, fundamentally, either in nature (*ṭabʿ*) or in position (*vaḍʿ*). The principle of nature applies in cases whose particulars conform to the intellects (*ʿoqūl*) of people of insight and the experience of men of sagacity, unvarying and unchanging with the variations of ages or the revolutions in modes of conduct and traditions. These correspond with the divisions of Practical Philosophy already mentioned. Where the principle lies in position, if the cause of the position be the agreed opinion of the community thereon, one speaks of *Manners* (*ādāb*) *and Customary Rules* (*rosūm*); if the cause of the position be, however, the exigency of the opinion of a great man, fortified by divine assistance, such as a prophet or an imam, one speaks of *Divine Laws* (*navāmīs-e elāhī*). The latter are further subdivided into three kinds: that which refers to each soul individually, e.g. devotions (*ʿebādāt*) and the statutory injunctions (*aḥkām*); that which refers to the inhabitants of dwellings in association, such as marriages and other transactions; that which refers to the inhabitants of cities and regions, e.g. penal laws and government. This type is under the title of the *Science of Jurisprudence*

[12]It is to be noted that even in his new preamble Ṭūsī used some typically Ismāʿīlī concepts and terminology. He praises God as the creator of man who, in his material nature, has "the brand of the World of Creation (*semat-e ʿālam-e khalqī*)" while, in his human form, he has been granted "the pattern of the World of Command (*terāz-e ʿālam-e amrī*)" (*Akhlāq-e Nāṣerī,* p. 33; Wickens, p. 23). The terms World of Command and World of Creation, signifying respectively the spiritual world brought forth initially by God through his command (*amr*) and the physical world of creation (*khalq*) produced secondarily through it, were of central importance in contemporary Nizārī teaching. Ṭūsī himself explains in his autiographical epistle (pp. 43–44) that according to the doctrine of the Taʿlīmīs all existent things have issued from God through something which the moderns (*motaʾakhkherān*) among them term his command or word (*kalema*). According to them it was the First Cause of the Intellect, which is the First Effect (*maʿlūl*). Through this doctrine they raised God above being the First Cause and countered the thesis of the philosophers that from the One could issue only one. The Ismāʿīlī point of view in this question had been upheld by ash-Shahrastānī in his *Wrestling Match.* There he rejected Avicenna's views that from God, the perfect One, only a single intellect could issue and that God is the unintentional necessitating cause (*mūjib*) of creation, and argued that all created things have an equally immediate relationship to God who is their giver of existence (*mūjid*) through what prophetic revelation terms his volition (*irāda*) and command (*amr*). In a crypto-Ismāʿīlī sermon ash-Shahrastānī also described the divine amr as the source (*maṣdar*) of creation which in turn was its manifestation (*maẓhar*) ("Aš-Šahrastānīs Streitschrift," pp. 256 f.) Ṭūsī accorded the thesis of creation through the divine amr prominent treatment in his Ismāʿīlī writings.

> (*feqh*). Now since the principle of this sort of action is position, it is liable to change, with revolutions in circumstances, with the pre-eminence of individual men, the prolongation of time, the disparity between epochs (*advār*), and the substitution of peoples and dynasties. This category thus falls, as regards the particular, outside the divisions of Philosophy, for the speculation of a philosopher is confined to examining the propositions of intellects and investigating the universalities of things, and these are not touched by decay or transcience, nor are they obliterated or replaced according to the obliteration of peoples and the severance of dynasties. From the summary standpoint, however, it does enter into the questions of Practical Philosophy. . . .[13]

Ethics and the divine law thus deal with the same subject matter, "the principles of beneficial works and virtuous acts." Ethics is, however, a rational science based on universal human nature and is therefore not subject to change. The divine law, on the other hand, is, just like conventional manners and rules of custom, "laid down" or posited, evidently not entirely on abstract rational grounds, and thus is changeable with changing ages and circumstances. Ṭūsī does not explain in this passage how the changeable law is interrelated with the unchangeable ethics, both dealing with the same subject matter. It is evident, however, that he, like the philosophers in general, considered the divine law as agreeing in substance with the principles of rational ethics. There could be no conflict between them; rather, the divine law must in some way embody these principles. Elsewhere, after explaining the Aristotelian doctrine that justice (*ᶜadālat*), implying equilibrium (*eᶜtedāl*) which is the "umbra of unicity," is the cardinal virtue of ethics. Ṭūsī explains, following closely his source, Miskawayh's *Tahdhīb:* "The determiner of the middle-point in every case, so that by knowledge thereof the repulsion of (other) things may be effected in equilibrium, is the Divine Law. Thus, in reality, the positor of equality and justice is the Divine Law, for God (exalted be mention of Him!) is the source of unicity."[14] Further on he states, again following Miskawayh: "Justice is a psychical affection, from which proceeds strict adherence to the Divine Law; for the Divine Law is the determiner of quantities, the specifier of positions and middle-points."[15]

In spite of its divine origin, however, the law ranks below the philosophical ethics on the human value scale leading to supreme felicity. Ṭūsī thus states, elaborating freely on his source, Miskawayh's *Tahdhīb:*

[13] *Akhlāq-e Nāṣerī,* pp. 45–46; Wickens, pp. 28–29. Ṭūsī's source in this section appears to be, as suggested by Dāneshpazhūh, Avicenna's *Risāla fī aqsām al-ᶜulum,* whose discussion, however, is much more summary.

[14] *Akhlāq-e Nāṣerī,* p. 133; Wickens, p. 97. Miskawayh, *Tahdhīb al-akhlāq,* ed. Qusṭanṭīn Zuraiq (Beirut, 1966), p. 115.

[15] *Akhlāq-e Nāṣerī,* p. 143; Wickens, p. 104. Miskawayh, *Tahdhīb,* pp. 125 f.

> The First Tutor, to the whole community, is the Divine Law in general; while the Second Tutor, to the possessor of distinction and the whole minds among them, is Philosophy in particular. So, by these degrees, they may arrive at the ascending ranks of perfection. Accordingly, it is incumbent on both mother and father to bring their children first of all into bondage to the Divine Law, and to reform their uses by various sorts of governance and discipline. . . . In sum, they should, by compulsion or free choice, so hold them to praiseworthy arts and approved uses as to make them habitual. When they attain perfection of the intellect, they will enjoy the fruits thereof; and they will understand, in all cogency, that the straight path and the right road are the ones to which they have been held; and if they are prepared for a greater favor, a solider felicity, with ease they will arrive thereat: if Almighty God will, He being the Guardian of Success.[16]

How do the philosophical views so far recorded by Ṭūsī, largely in agreement with Miskawayh, accord with the doctrine of the Islamic schools and sects? They were incompatible with the predominant position of Sunni Traditionalism as well as Ashᶜarism which does not admit a rational, unchangeable ethics independent of the divine law. Rather, it views ethics as an integral part of the imposed divine law and as solely derived from it. Thus ethics is subject to change with the change of the divine law, though the sharīᶜa of Islam, the most perfect and final of divine laws, would last unchanged until the end of the world. There was no basic conflict between the views presented by Ṭūsī and the position of the Muᶜtazila. They, too, affirmed the existence of a rational basis of ethics independent of revelation and held that the divine law must necessarily conform to it. Twelver Shiᶜis with their Muᶜtazilī theology thus might have read the *Tahdhīb al-akhlāq* of the Twelver Shiᶜi philosopher Miskawayh with some sympathy, noting his unambiguous support of the sharīᶜa and of the rightful imam as its upholder and just king.

The Ismāᶜīlī attitude towards the law was more complex. The Ismāᶜīlīs agreed with the Muslims in general that some of the prophets of the past had brought different divine laws, all of which had been superseded by the sharīᶜa of Islam brought by Muḥammad, whom they viewed as the inaugurator of the sixth prophetic era. Yet Ismāᶜīlīsm has always, though in practice to widely varying degrees, been characterized by an inherent antinomianism. Even those Ismāᶜīlīs who unreservedly affirmed the continued validity of the sharīᶜa of Islam believed that in the seventh prophetic era, that of the Qāʾim, it would be abrogated or, at any rate, fall gradually out of practice.[17]

[16] *Akhlāq-e Nāṣerī,* pp. 105 f.; Wickens, p. 77. Miskawayh, *Tahdhīb,* p. 35.

[17] The latter was the view of Ḥamīd ad-Dīn al-Kirmānī. See W. Madelung, "Das Imamat in der frühen ismailitischen Lehre," *Der Islam,* 37 (1961), 125.

The Qāʾim would not bring a new law but a purely spiritual message fully revealing the unchanging inner core of all prophetic messages which had so far remained hidden under their outward shell.

Among the Nizārī Ismāʿīlīs, Ḥasan-e Ṣabbāḥ had in his argumentation for the doctrine of taʿlīm emphasized the autonomous authority of each imam in independence from his predecessors. His theory was soon to acquire great practical significance. Imam Ḥasan ʿalā dhikrihi s-salām in 559/1164 proclaimed the Resurrection (*qiyāma*) and abrogated the Islamic sharīʿa. His grandson Jalāl ad-Dīn Ḥasan (607–618/1210–1221), known among non-Ismāʿīlīs as the New-Muslim (Naumosolmān), repudiated the qiyāma teaching, publicly cursed his predecessors, and imposed the sharīʿa in its Shāfiʿī form on his followers. They obediently accepted his orders as those of the infallible imam as they had earlier accepted the qiyāma. Jalāl ad-Dīn's son, ʿAlāʾ ad-Dīn Muḥammad, the imam at the time of Ṭūsī's writing, again relaxed the application of the sharīʿa without formally abolishing it. The Ismāʿīlī teaching establishment was called upon to explain and justify these momentous changes in the conduct of the imams and their administration of the divine law. The new teaching is known to us chiefly from the Ismāʿīlī writings of Ṭūsī himself. In his *Rawḍat at-taslīm* he explained that the qiyāma proclaimed by Ḥasan ʿalā dhikrihi s-salām had come about the middle of the millennium of the era of Muḥammad and set the pattern for the final qiyāma at the end of it.[18] The reimposition of the sharīʿa by Jalāl ad-Dīn was a return to a period of concealment (*satr*) when the truth is hidden under the shell of the law, in contrast to the qiyāma when it is unveiled and visible to all. In the era of Muḥammad periods of satr and qiyāma might alternate according to the decision of each imam, since every imam was a potential Qāʾim. These changes and contradictions in the conduct of the imams were, however, merely in appearance and in accordance with the circumstances of the time since the imams were in their true essence one and identical. This latter doctrine Ṭūsī took from the *Sacred Articles* of Ḥasan ʿalā dhikrihi s-salām.[19] In his autobiographical letter[20] Ṭūsī went so far as to affirm that the rightful imam might at different times manifest himself in different forms to mankind, might bring a different communication, reveal another truth, or lay down another sharīʿa without any change of his legitimacy since he was ever exalted above change and modification. The imam thus was fully sovereign over the sharīʿa.

These ideas, entirely foreign to most Islamic thought, are distinctly reflected in the *Nasirean Ethics*. Discussing the opinions of the philosophers

[18] W. Ivanow, *The Rawḍatu't-Taslīm Commonly Called Taṣawwurāt by Naṣīru'd-dīn Ṭūsī* (Leiden, 1950); see especially pp. 67 f. and 115–175.

[19] *Rawḍatu't-Taslīm,* pp. 130 f. Hodgson (*Order of Assassins,* p. 59) seems to be mistaken in attributing the quotation to Ḥasan-e Ṣabbāḥ.

[20] *Majmūʿa,* p. 52.

concerning man's obligations towards God, Miskawayh had mentioned two views of the modern (i.e., Muslim) philosophers about the duties comprised in worship. The first describes these duties, basically derived from the sharīʿa and traditional creeds, under three headings. The second starts with the brief definition: "Worship of God consists in true belief, sound utterance, and upright action,"[21] and then explains action in detail, again in terms of the duties of the Muslim under the sharīʿa. No difference in substance is implied, and both views support the integral implementation of the sharīʿa. In translating Miskawayh's text, Ṭūsī, however, introduces the second view with the words: "Of these (philosophers), a group more akin to the men of discernment, have said that the worship of Almighty God consists in three things: true belief, correct utterance, and upright action."[22] He omits Miskawayh's detailed description of action and substitutes the following significant passage: "The detailed implementation of each item, at any moment of time and on any occasion, and in any circumstance and regard, will vary as the prophets and the scholars of independent legal judgment (*ʿolamā-ye mojtahed*), who are the heirs of the prophets, may expound; and the mass of mankind, to keep the Commandment of the Truth (exalted is His glory!), is under the obligation to submit to them and to conform to their course." Ṭūsī is quoting *ḥadīth* in referring to the scholars of *ijtihād* as the heirs of the prophets.[23] But he does not mean the mujtahids in the technical sense. Rather, the imams are the heirs of the prophets and they, in succession to the prophets, have full authority over the divine law to expound it in accordance with the change of time and circumstances. Already in his initial definition of practical philosophy Ṭūsī had mentioned the imam together with the prophet as the imposer of the divine law in accordance with the "exigency of his opinion."

Most explicitly expressed, however, are these ideas in the section on politics based on the political philosophy of al-Fārābī with its Platonic background. Here Ṭūsī found a discussion of the necessity of change in the divine law and its application by the philosopher-kings in accordance with the requirements of the time yet without incoherence in the unity of their purpose. The immediate source of the following passages of the *Nasirean Ethics,* and how closely Ṭūsī followed it in them, is not known. That he saw them as confirming the Ismāʿīlī views which he expounded elsewhere in his writings of this period would be obvious even if he had not drawn the readers' attention to the agreement. After explaining that government depends partly

[21] Miskawayh, *Tahdhīb,* pp. 122 f.

[22] *Akhlāq-e Nāṣerī,* p. 141; Wickens, p. 103.

[23] In its common form the ḥadīth speaks only of the scholars (*ʿulamāʾ*) as the heirs of the prophets. For a Shiʿi version, attributed to imam Jaʿfar aṣ-Ṣādiq, see al-Kulainī, *al-Uṣūl min al-Kāfī,* ed. ʿA. A. al-Ghaffārī (Tehran, 1388/1968), p. 32, n. 2, where the scholars are identified with the imams.

on enactments (*auḍāᶜ*), as with contracts and transactions, and partly on rational judgments (*aḥkām-e ᶜaqlī*), as with the management of a kingdom or the administration of a city, Ṭūsī continues:

> But no one would be able to undertake either of these two categories without a preponderance of discrimination and a superiority in knowledge, for such a man's precedence over others without the occasion of some particularity would call for strife and altercation. Thus, in determining the enactments there is a need for a person distinguished from others by divine inspiration, in order that they should follow him. Such a person, in the terminology of the Ancients, was called the Possessor of the Law (*ṣāḥeb-e nāmūs*), and his enactments the Divine Law; the Moderns refer to him as the Religious Lawgiver (*shāreᶜ*), and to his enactments as the sharīᶜa. Plato, in the Fifth Discourse of the *Book of Politics,* has referred to this class thus: "They are the possessors of mighty and surpassing powers." Aristotle, again, has said: "They are the ones for whom God has greater concern."
>
> Now, in determining judgments, there is a need also for a person who is distinguished from others by divine support, so that he may be able to accomplish their perfection. Such a person, in the terminology of the Ancients, was called an Absolute King, and his judgments the Craft of Kingship; the Moderns refer to him as the Imam, and to his function as the Imamate. Plato calls him the Regulator (*modabber*) of the World, while Aristotle uses the term Civic Man, i.e. that man, and his like, by whose existence the ordering of civilized life is effected.[24]

Here Ṭūsī adds: "In the terminology of some, the first of these persons is called the Speaker (*nāṭeq*), and the second the Foundation (*asās*)." It is purely Ismāᶜīlī terminology, referring to the Messenger Prophet, the bringer of a law at the beginning of each prophetic cycle, and his successor, the founder of the imamate. He continues:

> It must be established that the term "king" in this place is not that of someone possessing a cavalcade, a retinue or a realm: what is meant, rather, is one truly deserving of kingship, even though outwardly no one pays him any attention. If someone other than he be carrying on the management of affairs, tyranny and disorder become widespread.
>
> In short, not every age and generation has need of a Possessor of the Law, for one enactment suffices for the people of many periods; but the world does require a Regulator in every age, for if management ceases, order is taken away likewise, and the survival of the species in

[24]*Akhlāq-e Nāṣerī,* pp. 253 f.; Wickens, pp. 191–192.

> the most perfect manner cannot be realized. The Regulator undertakes to preserve the Law and obliges men to uphold its prescriptions; his is the authority of jurisdiction over the particulars of the Law in accordance with the best interest of every day and age.[25]

The imams thus have sovereignty over the divine law to apply its particulars in accordance with circumstances. The point is reinforced and developed in a later passage. Ṭūsī states with respect to the people of al-Fārābī's Virtuous City:

> Their rulers, who are the regulators of the world, have control of the enactments of laws (*auḍāᶜ-e navāmīs*) and of the most expedient measures in daily life: this, by modes of control that are congenial and appropriate to time and circumstance, a particular control in the enactments of laws and a universal control in the enactments of expedient measures. This is the reason for the interdependence of faith and kingship, as expressed by the Emperor of the Iranians, the Philosopher of the Persians, Ardashīr Bābak: "Religion and kingship are twins, neither being complete without the other." Religion is the base and kingship the support: just as a foundation without support avails nothing, while a support without foundation falls into ruin, so religion without kingship is profitless, and kingship without faith is easily broken.
>
> However numerous this class may be, i.e. kings and regulators of the Virtuous City, whether at one time or different times, nevertheless their rule is the rule of one individual, for their regard is to one end, namely ultimate felicity, and they are directed to one object of desire, namely the true destination (*maᶜād*). So the control exercized by a successor on the rulings of his predecessor, in accordance with best interest, is not in opposition to him but represents a perfection of his law. Thus, if the successor had been present in the former time, he would have instituted that same law; and if the predecessor were at hand in the later time, he would effect the selfsame control, for the way of intelligence is one. A confirmation of this argument is to be found in the words reportedly uttered by Jesus (peace be upon him!): "I have not come to cancel the Torah, but I have come to perfect it." Control and disagreement and discord, however, are conceived by the community who are Image Worshippers, not Seers of the Truth.[26]

[25] The addition is missing in many manuscripts and may have been removed by Ṭūsī in his later revision of the text. See the editors' annotation to p. 253 of *Akhlāq-e Nāṣerī* on p. 390.

[26] *Akhlāq-e Nāṣerī,* p. 285; Wickens, p. 215. Dāneshpazhūh (introd. to *Akhlāq-e Moḥtashamī,* p. 22) suggests that the passage is based on al-Fārābī's *Talkhīṣ nawāmīs Aflāṭūn,* ed. F. Gabrieli (London, 1952), p. 35. There is, however, no close parallel.

The prophets and their successors, the imams, thus are the philosopher-kings, the rulers of the Virtuous City, and the regulators of the world. As such they are the controllers and administrators of the law which they legislate with divine assistance and apply in accordance with the requirements of the time. They are also, however, the guides and instructors of man on the path to supreme felicity, the ultimate goal of ethics. In Nizārī Ismāᶜīlī terms, they were the dispensers of taᶜlīm.

In Miskawayh's *Tahdhīb* Ṭūsī found a discussion of the natural obstacles on the way to perfect felicity ending with the statement: "Because of this, men are in frequent need for rectifiers and trainers (*muqawwimīn, muthaqqifīn*), tutors and directors (*muʾaddibīn, musaddidīn*). For those outstanding natural qualities which drift by themselves, without advice, to felicity are difficult to come by and can only be realized over lengthy times and prolonged periods."[27] In his rendering, Ṭūsī identified the rectifiers of the soul with the prophets and imams and transformed the passage giving it an entirely new significance. Man in his quest for perfection, he explains,

> is in a need for prophets and philosophers, imams, guides (*hodāt*), tutors and teachers (*moᶜallemīn*), who should—some graciously, others with severity—prevent his facing towards affliction and disaster (in which there is no need for great effort or movement, every rest and lack of movement being indeed sufficient in that sense); and who should turn his face towards eternal felicity (on which must be expended both effort and solicitude, this goal being unattainable without movement of the mind along the path of truth, and the acquisition of virtue). Thus, through leadership and direction, discipline and teaching (*taᶜlīm*), men arrive at the sublimest rank of existence. God prosper us in what He loves and approves, and lead us aside from the pursuit of passion![28]

As the supreme teachers of spiritual truths which perfect the soul and guide it to ultimate felicity, the prophets and imams are entitled to a love, obedience, and veneration which are second only to those of God. In his chapter on the different kinds of love, Miskawayh had argued that the love of the pupil of philosophy for the philosopher is above the love of the child for his parents and below the love of man for God.[29] Ṭūsī replaces the philosopher by the teacher and says:

> The pretenders to love of God are many, but the true practitioners among them are few, nay fewer than few. Obedience and veneration

[27] Miskawayh, *Tahdhīb,* p. 71.

[28] *Akhlāq-e Nāṣerī,* pp. 64 f.; Wickens, p. 48.

[29] Miskawayh, *Tahdhīb,* pp. 148 f.

are never absent from such true love: "Few of My servants are grateful."[30] Love of parents follows this love in rank, and no other love attains the rank of these two, save that of the teacher in the student's heart, this latter love being intermediate in rank between the two aforementioned loves. The reason for this is as follows: the first (type of) love is at the very extremity of nobility and grandeur inasmuch as the Object of love is the cause of existence and of the grace consequent on existence; the second (type of) love is related to this in that the father is the sensible reason and the proximate cause (of these); teachers, however, in the nurture of the souls, may be equated with fathers in the nurture of bodies; again, from the standpoint that they are the completers of existence and the perpetuators of essences, they imitate the Primary Cause, and from the standpoint that their nurture is a branch on the root of existence, they may be likened to fathers. Thus, love of them is inferior to the first (type of) love, but above the second, for their nurture is a ramification upon the root of existence, but nobler than the nurture of fathers. In truth, the teacher is a corporeal master and a spiritual master, his rank in veneration being below that of the Primary Cause but above that of human fathers.

Alexander was asked whether he loved his father or his teacher the more, to which he replied: "My teacher, for my father was the cause of my transitory life, whereas my teacher was a cause of my life everlasting." Thus, the right of the teacher over that of the father is in the measure of the superiority in rank of the soul over the body, and this proportion must be preserved in the love and veneration shown to him as compared with the father. Likewise, the love of the teacher for the student in the way of good is superior to that of the father for the son in the same proportion, for the teacher nurtures on complete virtue and sustains with pure wisdom, so that his relation to the father is like that of the soul to the body.[31]

Ismāʿīlī readers at least could be in no doubt about the primary identity of these teachers.

In the last decade of his life, three decades after the *Nasirean Ethics*, Ṭūsī wrote a treatise on Sufi ethics entitled *The Attributes of the Illustrious* (*Ausāf al-ashrāf*).[32] In the introduction he explained that, after composing the

[30] Qurʾān, 34.13.

[31] *Akhlāq-e Nāṣerī*, pp. 270 f.; Wickens, pp. 204–205.

[32] Ed. Naṣrollah Taqavī (Berlin, 1306/1929). Another ethical work by Ṭūsī, *Akhlāq-e Mohtashamī*, is of no immediate relevance here. It is a collection of ethical texts and aphorisms taken from the Qurʾān, ḥadīth, statements of the imams, dāʿīs, and philosophers begun by Ṭūsī's Ismāʿīlī patron, the Muḥtasham Nāṣer ad-Dīn, and completed and translated into Persian by Ṭūsī. Another ethical treatise ascribed to Ṭūsī, *Goshāyeshnāme* (ed. M. T. Dāneshpazhūh, in the volume *Do resāle dar akhlāq* [Tehran, 1341/1964]), does not appear authentic.

*Nasirean Ethics,* which expounded the noble character traits and satisfactory conduct according to the way of the philosophers, he had wished to prepare a précis elucidating the path of the saints and the conduct of the people of spiritual cognition built upon rational and traditional foundations. Multiple occupations, however, had prevented him until the vizier Shams ad-Dīn Muḥammad Jovainī invited him to carry out the project.[33]

The *Auṣāf al-ashrāf* stands apart from Ṭūsī's other writings. Most of his books and treatises of his later age dealt with philosophy and astronomy or defended Twelver Shiᶜi theology and religious doctrine. The *Auṣāf al-ashrāf* is his only work in the Sufi style. Ṭūsī briefly describes the states and stations of the mystic on the path from faith (*īmān*) to union (*vaḥda*) and extinction (*fanā*ᵓ) of the self in God in traditional terms. The work thus belongs to the classical school of Sufism; there are no apparent traces of the speculative mysticism elaborated by Ibn al-ᶜArabī a generation before Ṭūsī. It represents a Sufism of the heart rather than the mind. The Shiᶜi creed of the author finds expression only in the formulas of benediction at the beginning and end of the treatise.[34] Imam Muḥammad al-Bāqir is described in an edifying narrative as a Sufi having reached the state of contentment (*reḍā*) while the Companion Jābir al-Anṣārī was still in the preceding state of patience (*ṣabr*)[35] The list of divine attributes mentioned is Ashᶜarī, and the definition of faith as excluding works, Murjiᵓī Ḥanafī,[36] both in conflict with Muᶜtazilī Shiᶜi doctrine. The integral practice of the sharīᶜa is enjoined unequivocally. Concerning the state of union (*etteḥād*) Ṭūsī emphasizes that it does not imply, as some men lacking insight hold, that the mystic becomes one with God but rather that he will become seeing through the eye of divine self-revelation and, as he sees everything to be from Him, will see nothing but Him. Ṭūsī then justifies the famous utterance of al-Ḥallāj "I am the Truth" as not implying a claim to divinity.[37] Before Ṭūsī al-Ḥallāj had universally been condemned by Twelver Shiᶜis.

How does this Sufi treatise relate to Ṭūsī's personal concerns and aspirations? Was he in his old age attracted to the path of a mysticism of the heart turning away from his earlier intellectual pursuits and religious commitments? There is no evidence that he ever became a practicing Sufi; and in referring to the *Nasirean Ethics* he did not distance himself from his earlier work on philosophical ethics. Why did he feel then both the competence and the call to write a treatise on Sufi ethics, even before he was urged to do so by the vizier?

[33] *Auṣāf al-ashrāf,* p. 2.
[34] Ibid., pp. 1, 69.
[35] Ibid., pp. 42 f.
[36] Ibid., pp. 6 f.
[37] Ibid., pp. 66 f.

After his escape from the Ismāʿīlīs, Ṭūsī had, as was natural, rejoined the Twelver Shiʿi community into which he had been born. In the catastrophic and chaotic conditions during and after the Mongol conquest, he, more than anyone else, was in a position to protect its members' lives, property, and interests, a position he used fully. He also gave the community his moral support, maintaining close relations with some of its leading religious scholars and writing treatises expounding and defending Twelver Shiʿi theology and belief at their request. He rejoined the Twelver Shiʿi community as a philosopher as he had earlier joined the Ismāʿīlīs. Yet he was no longer seeking the muʿallim, the supreme teacher who could guide him to perfect and transcend his philosophical faith. He had now become the foremost philosopher of his time. In the Twelver Shiʿi community, the position of a supreme teacher could, in the absence of the Twelfth Imam, only fall to him. Ṭūsī himself was the Master (*khᵛāje*), the King of Philosophers (*malek al-ḥokamā*), the Teacher of Mankind (*ostād al-bashar*) as he was now commonly addressed.

In writing theological treatises for the Twelver Shiʿi community, Ṭūsī may well have remembered the ḥadīth quoted by him in the *Nasirean Ethics:* "We (the prophets) speak to men in the measure of their intelligences!"[38] It is not likely that he had changed his earlier judgment of kalām that it merely served to defend inherited creeds. It was his own inherited creed which he thus defended now. But he also believed that, as he put it in his new introduction to the *Nasirean Ethics,* philosophy "bears no relation to the agreement or disagreement of school or sect or denomination." Those Sunni scholars in the Mamlūk west who described him as an inveterate hater of Sunni Islam and accused him of maliciously encouraging to kill the last Abbasid caliph of Baghdad certainly failed to do him justice.[39] In the Mongol east, Sunni biographers wrote about him with respect and admiration and Sunni scholars studied, and wrote commentaries on, his main compendium of theology. Among his associates, correspondants, and students were numerous Sunni scholars.

Ṣadr ad-Dīn Qūnavī, the most famous disciple of Ibn al-ʿArabī, also exchanged letters with Ṭūsī, and some of them are extant. There Qūnavī puts the questions, and Ṭūsī gives the answers; and although Ṭūsī modestly describes himself as a neophyte (*morīd*) and a seeker to learn (*mostafīd*) in relation to the eminent Sufi sheikh, he puts the latter in fact more in the

[38]*Akhlāq-e Nāṣerī,* p. 283; Wickens, p. 214.

[39]See the accusations of Ibn Taimiyya, Ibn Qayyim al-Jauziyya, al-Subkī, and others quoted by Modarres Reḍavī, *Aḥvāl o āthār-e . . . Khᵛāja Naṣīr ad-Dīn* (Tehran, 1334/1957), pp. 46–49. Ṭūsī's diversion of the religious endowments to the support of philosophy and sciences, for which he was also criticized, certainly was detrimental to Sunni interests in particular. His measures in this regard were, however, merely an aspect of the disestablishment of Sunnism as the official religion by the Mongols.

place of the pupil.[40] It is thus not surprising that he felt competent to compose a treatise on the Sufi path. Both he and the vizier Jovainī, a Sunni and firm supporter of Islam, must have sensed the growing tide of Sufi sentiment throughout Islam, which was to reach its peak in the Mongol age. They must have been aware that Sufism, if anything, could break down the barriers between schools and sects and unite all Muslims under the banner of the great Sufi orders. Ṭūsī thus conceived his treatise on Sufi ethics as a complement, addressed to the common Muslim, to his philosophical ethics, addressed to the elite. He wrote it in simple, uncontroversial terms widely acceptable among Muslims of all creeds, under the motto: "We speak to men in the measure of their intelligences." The *Auṣāf al-ashrāf* did not reflect a development in Ṭūsī's views on ethics. It reflected his awareness of the signs and needs of the time.

[40] See Modarres Reḍavī, *Aḥvāl,* pp. 270–277. For Ibn Taimiyya's view of the correspondence see T. Michel, "Ibn Taymiyya's Critique of *Falsafa,*" *Hamdard Islamicus,* 6 (1938), 12.

# ETHICS AND THE QUR'ĀN: COMMUNITY AND WORLD VIEW

FREDERICK M. DENNY
University of Colorado, Boulder

The first thing that must be said about ethics and the sacred book of the Muslims is that the Qur'ān is neither a work of systematic theology nor an essay in the science of moral discourse. Like the Bible of the Jews and Christians, the Qur'ān is a sourcebook for faith and order and not a textbook of definition and regulation. Because of this, the Qur'ān is not to be equated with the subsequent developments of Islamic thought and practice connected with theology, law, or ethics. There is, however, a persistent tradition or pattern of thinking down through the Islamic ages which insists that the fundamental authority in all matters is the revelation as it is contained in the Qur'ān. But often the Qur'ān has been the prisoner of the interpreters rather than their source and guide. Perhaps it is because of this that the Qur'ān has not been as prominent a source for Islamic ethics as might be expected by someone coming to the subject for the first time within the Islamic context.

Over the past twenty or so years several studies of Qur'ānic ethics have appeared in English which have focused on the terminology of the Qur'ān. Two major works by Toshihiko Izutsu have quite thoroughly explored the semantic range of Qur'ān terms and concepts bearing on the subject.[1] The painstakingly detailed work of Daud Rahbar, *God of Justice,* went in a different direction to find the central theme of the Qur'ān and to demonstrate how the other themes were subordinate to the divine justice.[2] A more recent study by Fazlur Rahman[3] implicitly rejects the Rahbar

Unless otherwise indicated, the Qur'ān translation used in quotes is that of Richard Bell, *The Qur'ān* (2 vols.; Edinburgh: T. & T. Clark, 1937; repr. 1960).

[1] *Ethico-Religious Concepts in the Qur'ān* (Montreal: McGill University Press, 1966), *God and Man in the Koran: Semantics of the Koranic Weltanschauung* (Tokyo: The Keio Institute of Cultural and Linguistic Studies, 1964).

[2] *God of Justice: A Study of the Ethical Doctrines of the Qur'ān* (Leiden: E. J. Brill, 1960).

[3] *Major Themes of the Qur'ān* (Minneapolis and Chicago: Bibliotheca Islamica, 1980).

thesis by showing how God's mercy creates, informs, and animates the universe. In Rahman's profound discussion in *Major Themes of the Qur'ān* the divine justice is certainly not minimized, but neither is it held up as the final attribute of God. A much more recent article-length study by George Hourani, "Ethical Presuppositions of the Qur'ān,"[4] clearly and convincingly demonstrates that the Qur'ān does teach that "ethical value has an objective reality and is not reducible in essence to the commands and prohibitions of God." Hourani is quick to affirm that "the chief source of ethical knowledge is revelation, particularly the Qur'ān."[5] Izutsu, Rahman, and Hourani all hold that the Qur'ān is the fundamental source of authentic Islamic value formation, including ethics, and that it is far more subtle and nuanced in both its prescriptive and descriptive dimensions than the simplistic ethical voluntarism of the later Sunni law schools, which have for better or worse dominated and, to specify what I said earlier, imprisoned the revelation.

Although the working out of a detailed Qur'ānic ethics has yet to be accomplished for the modern period, the semantic and theological and presuppositional foundations for such a task have been essentially completed in the work of Izutsu, Rahman, and Hourani. The last scholar has profitably reopened the whole Muʿtazilite approach to Qur'ānic ethics, and it will be interesting to see whether and to what extent other scholars—whether Muslim or not—will be inspired to return to a rationalist interpretation and application of the revelation. It is not my goal to rehearse further what has already been achieved in the way of ethical analysis of the Qur'ān. I will not attempt to discern once again the basic categories of value or to demonstrate the continuities, transitions, and transformations that occurred between the Jāhiliyya and Islam's establishment as the dominant religious and value system in Arabia. These tasks have fairly well been completed and what remains to be done is on the more specific levels of how the Qur'ān was itself appropriated and applied within the developing elaboration of law and theology over the early Islamic centuries. But this enterprise is both too ambitious and too detailed to pursue in the present context. What I have set as my task here is to show that Qur'ānic ethics can profitably be viewed as the basic value dimension of a living, dynamic community ideal whose structure and function are adumbrated in the Qur'ān overall and in certain respects specifically prescribed. What I am talking about is the Ummah, whose essential characteristics are laid out in the Qur'ān and put into a mythic and symbolic context that moves from Abraham, through Moses, to the bold affirmation that the Muslims are the "best community" of all time.[6]

[4] *The Muslim World,* 70, no. 1 (January 1980), 1–28.

[5] Ibid., p. 25.

[6] See Frederick M. Denny, "The Meaning of *Ummah* in the Qur'ān," *History of Religions,* 15, no. 1 (August 1975), 34–70. In this paper, as elsewhere, I have distinguished between

The beginnings of the Ummah as an independent and encompassing human social and political order under religious authority are in Medina, although the indispensable antecedents are to be found in the small, exclusive movement of Mecca, which as a religious reformation failed (in the short run) but which, enduring persecution, became prepared for the challenges to come. The important Constitution of Medina, which has been transmitted to us by Ibn Isḥāq (in his *Sīra*) provides a rudimentary outline of the type of agreement reached among the parties of the oasis at Yathrib toward the end of a stable and secure public order. The Constitution is of the greatest value for any effort of historical reconstruction, for it specifies in a convenantal, and, in fact, a legally contractual sense what the Qur᾽ān tends to treat in an oracular and disjointed manner concerning the specific articles, sanctions, and parties of the arrangement.[7] The Qur᾽ān, however, does in its unique way provide the authentic, original background and theory for what it meant for Muhammad and his people to establish a new order.

The Ummah, as we should define it today, is highly influenced and conditioned by post-Qur᾽ānic developments, interpretations, and constructions, blended with later cultural, political, juridical, and religious elements. Islam and the Ummah, as has often been said, are both *dīn* and *dawlah,* "religion" and "state," under God's legislation, the holy *sharīᶜah,* which prescribes how the believers shall live in community obediently and successfully and how they shall anticipate their destinies. The Ummah has in all times and places been regarded by Muslims as one of the central coordinates of their belief and of their social and political well-being. It is a complex, dynamic reality which by its charismatic nature cannot be fully defined within the Qur᾽ānic context alone. A comprehensive understanding of the Ummah in history and in the present requires a grasp of the sweep of Islamic experience and self-interpretation of profound depth and breadth.

The Ummah is the entire Muslim community as it exists at any point in time, considered on the simplest level of generalization. An illustration has been fashioned, in triangular terms, with the angles Culture, Doctrine, and History all joined by sides which together encompass the concept of the Ummah. It is interesting to observe the primacy of the sociological in a Muslim's own heuristic model.[8] The Ummah, then, is not simply the Muslim

Ummah as the Muslim community, and *ummah* as an Arabic technical term, which may refer to other communities, as well. In effect Ummah has become in recent years an English proper noun, at least among scholars of Islam. It is analogous to Church, for the Christian community, and Samgha, for the Buddhist monastic community.

[7] See Frederick M. Denny, "*Ummah* in the 'Constitution of Medina,'" *Journal of Near Eastern Studies,* 36, no. 1 (January 1977), 39–47. Also, by the same author, "Some Religio-Communal Terms and Concepts in the Qur᾽ān," *Numen,* 24, no. 1 (February 1977), 26–59, for a consideration of covenant and related topics.

[8] I was introduced to this model in a faculty seminar given by Professor Yusuf Ibish at Dartmouth College, Autumn 1966.

community in a gross empirical sense; it is the community being the community in specific ways. There is a normative quality inherent in it, because it is a holy community with a transcendent origin and purpose, enlivened and sustained by a transcendent power.

C. A. O. van Nieuwenhuijze has written of the "poly-interpretability" of the concept of the Ummah and the problems of definition of the term.[9] Muhammad was engaged in the virtual remaking of Arab society along the lines of religion, in which the converts, the Muslims, were called to be a community in which dīn would replace the traditional virtues and customs of Arab tribalism as value center and basis for social and political order. What W. Montgomery Watt has termed "tribal humanism"[10] (which was in fact giving way to the sometimes cruel and callous practices of an emerging mercantile order dominated by the Meccan oligarchy), based on kinship and traditional values, would be replaced by a religious orientation in which all Arabs and all mankind, potentially and ideally, would form the community, the Ummah of Islam. But this was not to occur in a sudden, drastic shift; a great struggle would ensue before religion would even superficially predominate in the Arabian Peninsula alone. Asserting that the new dispensation did not require a repudiation and dissolution of all former affinities and values, "a complete changeover of social *Angehörigkeit,*" van Nieuwenhuijze writes:

> ". . . *ummah* was the sort of word that could be given a new shade of meaning; it was also capable of further development subsequently."[11] After all, in order to attain longevity and achieve a lasting impact as one of the central coordinates of an ever-expanding community, a concept needs nothing more than poly-interpretability. Definitions are definitely less important. If the neologism ummah was to have any operational significance during the period (sc. in the process) of its formation, it must have been that of being the abstract entity (the rationalization, the concept) standing for (or symbolizing) the cohesion of all Muslims as Muslims, as a conscious cohesion made explicit. Once it had come into existence as an abstract entity, a living concept in its proper linguistic setting, it could, reversely, act as a force maintaining and stimulating this same cohesion. Therefore, symbol of cohesion and cohesive force all at once.[12]

If it assumes a great deal on the part of Muhammad as a conscious coiner of axial terms, the passage does make clear the peculiar quality of the term

[9] "The Ummah—an Analytic Approach," *Studia Islamica,* 10 (1959), 5–22.

[10] *Muhammad at Mecca* (Oxford: Oxford University Press, 1953), p. 24.

[11] Quoted from W. Montgomery Watt, *Muhammad at Medina* (Oxford: Oxford University Press, 1956), p. 240.

[12] "The Ummah—an Analytic Approach," p. 13.

"ummah" and some of its effects. The Muslim community is both a social, historical reality and an ideal toward which to strive. There is a sense of becoming entailed in it; it somehow is what it is becoming and becomes what it is, or rather becomes what and as it *intends*. Because the Ummah is an intentional, moral community, any definition must characterize it as both ideal and somewhat abstract as well as practical and functional: a "symbol of cohesion and cohesive force" at the same time, which at its truest and best reflects a community which is "in a bond of God, and a bond of the people" (3:112).

Although no suggestion is made that the specifically Qurʾānic doctrine of the Ummah exhausts its meaning, for it clearly does not, it is a valid project to consider the Ummah's germinal phases as a moral community in the Qurʾānic record. If the Qurʾān does not provide the sources or rationale for a complete understanding of the Ummah and Islamic ethics, it does contain the most authentic clues concerning their essentially religious orientation, which is markedly soteriological. If the Ummah, then, is more than a strictly Qurʾānic definition can encompass, taken even in a generously impressionistic sense, it is at the same time never less than what the Qurʾān holds it to be: the righteous community of *falāḥ* (better translated as "success" than "salvation"). Concerning this central aspect of Muslim reality, as in all the vital dimensions of Muslim self-understanding and interpretation, the Qurʾān is normative and regulative, although not descriptively exhaustive.

Muslims do not deny a soteriological dimension in their religion, although the terms "salvation" and "soteriology" are not commonly encountered in Muslim discourse. This fact does not mean that the concept is lacking, but simply that Western and especially Christian terminology, or Eastern and Buddhist terminology, for that matter, do not apply. In short, Islam does not embrace a strong rhetoric of salvation.[13] But the best proof of the centrality of the concept is found through the Qurʾān itself, which is deeply concerned with the human predicament and how we may be delivered from it or, to use a more characteristic Islamic expression, how we may "triumph" over it, how we may be among the "successful" (*al-mufliḥūn*), and receive saving "guidance" (*hudan, hidāya*) and avoid "loss."

There is, of course, no redemptorist soteriology in Islam, predicated on a fallen mankind as in Christianity, at least not in the Sunni tradition. And there is no doctrine of original sin,[14] although there is a clear sense of man's sinfulness and willful perversity in being ungrateful and insolent toward

[13] For a more detailed treatment, with references, see Frederick M. Denny, "The Problem of Salvation in the Qurʾān: Key Terms and Concepts," in A. H. Green, ed., *The Quest for an Islamic Humanism: Arabic and Islamic Studies in Memory of Mohamed al-Nowaihi,* in press.

[14] See Georges Anawati, "La notion de péché originel existe-elle dans l'Islam?" *Studia Islamica,* 30 (1970), 29–40.

God (a very common theme throughout the Qur᾿ān). If the Muslim's idea of sinfulness is not as radical in the ontological sense as a Christian doctrine inevitably and perhaps necessarily is, it may be that the evil ways of basically good people are even more mysterious. There is little to be gained theologically or scientifically by a search for the greater sin; but it is a reasonable activity to seek to understand the ways in which religious people have symbolized and internalized their sense of wrong and wrong-doing.

Muslim, or to be more specific, Qur᾿ānic ideas of salvation (the distinction is often necessary, as has already been suggested concerning the meaning of the Ummah itself) are characterized in very positive terms as entailing a successful outcome to life in this world, with happiness and the sense of being part of an upright and just fellowship uppermost in the minds of the believers. Although the present life may be just "a sport and a pastime" (6:32), and the world to come, *al-ākhirah,* with its promise of paradise or damnation, a keenly anticipated reality, there is a clear sense in which Muslim soteriology includes success, transformation, and reward in this life, too, particularly on the level of the Ummah (e.g., 3:103: "And remember Allah's favour unto you: how ye were enemies and He made friendship between your hearts so that ye became brothers by His grace; and (how) ye were upon the brink of an abyss of fire, and He did save you from it—Pickthall trans.). The optimistic linking of salvation as success with the very identity of the Muslim community is a result, in part, of the great achievements of Muhammad and his people. This fact is at the center of Islamic reflection on the Battle of Badr, in A.H. 2, (March 624 C.E.), when Muhammad and his greatly outnumbered band of Medinans carried the day against the invading Meccans. This day is called, in 8:42, *yaum al-furqān,* the "Day of Deliverance" or "Day of Discrimination," depending upon how the term *furqān* is interpreted here, for mere translation is not sufficient. On this great day was accomplished, in the words of Richard Bell, "the deliverance of the Muslims and their separation from the unbelievers, the assurance of divine approval, the establishment of the Muslims as a distinct community."[15]

The ethical dimension of the Qur᾿ānic message is very much intertwined with the vision of the holy community in its intimate relation with God and his Prophet. To be sure, the various and interconnected ritual, legal, social, and moral obligations and regulations are all part of a deontology in which obedience to God's will is fundamental, however inscrutable that will may be. But there is also a teleological dimension which envisions a people obeying God because He is good and seeking by means of a given natural constitution (*fiṭra*) to progress in the direction of felicity and common life as "the best community" yet brought forth for humankind. The Qurʿānic

[15]W. Montgomery Watt, *Bell's Introduction to the Qur᾿ān,* Islamic Surveys, 8 (Edinburgh: Edinburgh University Press, 1970), pp. 146–147.

ethic is neither wholly voluntaristic nor objective–rationalist. It is, in fact, covenantal and entails mutual rights and obligations within an unfolding and suspenseful historical process. — The remainder of this paper will explore this by means of three central themes which seem to me to bring together essential elements of the Qur'ān's ethical teachings as they relate to the community. The three themes are: (a) the Abrahamic component of Qur'ānic religion; (b) the concept of an *ummah muslimah;* and (c) the Muslims as the best ummah.

## (a) The Abrahamic Component

The spiritual and historical model for the Muslim ummah is Abraham.[16] In 16:120 and 121, obedience, *ḥanīfī* piety, and the abjuration of polytheism, together with thankfulness for God's blessings and bounty, ensure that one will be on "the straight path." Muhammad was told to follow the "religion" (*millah*) of Abraham (16:123) and this, in turn, would be the way for his people, who would follow the archetypal predecessors as the new, Arab, ummah muslimah. In 2:134 and 141 the Jews and Christians are told: "That is an *ummah* [i.e., Abraham through Jacob] which has passed away; to it what it has earned and to you what you have earned. And you will not be asked of what they used to do" (trans. adapted from Bell). The Muslims are commanded to follow the example of the primordial ummah of Abraham which was prior to and independent of the Jews and the Christians. But the new community would neither benefit from the good which the first ummah did (except as a model) nor be held liable for the bad; each was to be judged according to its own acts. This probably means that Abraham could not intercede in any way for the Muslims of Muhammad's time, on the one hand; on the other, it seems that God comforted the new Muslims by granting an entirely new beginning, but with the old and primordial value system.

So the Muslim ummah would not be tied to the past, although it certainly might be guided by it through the example of Abraham. Salvation history[17] is one in which God respects His creatures and does not doom the descendants of evil-doers nor reward those who only nominally follow such paradigms as Abraham. Thus neither the Jews nor the Christians had a

[16] For a thorough examination of Abrahamic dimensions of the Qur'ānic message, see Y. Moubarac, *Abraham dans le Coran,* Études Musulmanes, 5 (Paris: J. Vrin, 1958).

[17] While it could be objected that this term, from the German *Heilsgeschichte,* is so freighted with Christian biblical-theological assumptions as to be irrelevant to Islam, I would argue that it is a useful and appropriate phrase from the Qur'ānic perspective, so long as no specific theological position is assumed along with it. The Qur'ān views itself as the final record of God's ways with humankind, authenticating the scriptural warnings and promises to former peoples and correcting their errors and distortions so as to keep the original and enduring message intact.

special claim on salvation or success simply because they were descended from Abraham. The same is true for the Muslims of Muhammad: They must follow the right path and stand before God's judgment with no appeal beyond their acts and their belief.

> They [the Jews and Christians] say: "Be ye Jews or Christians and ye will be guided"; Say (thou): "Nay, the creed [*millah*] of Abraham, who was a Ḥanīf, but was not one of the idolaters." Say ye [O Muslims]: "We have believed in Allah and what has been sent down to us, and what has been down to Abraham and Ishmael and Isaac and Jacob and the Patriarchs and what has been given to Moses and Jesus and what has been given to the prophets from their Lord, making no distinction between any of them; and to Him are we submissive [*wa nahnu lahu muslimūn*]. So if they believe in something like what ye believe in, they have been guided; but if they turn away, it is they who are in schism; Allah will attend to them for thee, He is the one who hears and knows." (2:135–137)

The Qurʾān certainly does not deny "success" to peoples other than those to whom Muhammad was sent; but schism and turning aside from the primordial religion are damnable acts. More than that, the claim is made in the foregoing passage that the Muslims believe not in Abraham's way simply, but "in Allah and what has been sent down to us," as well as the revelations to prior prophets of God. So Muhammad connects his people horizontally and humanly with the past back to Abraham, and vertically in the present with God in a direct relationship. This is a real *Heilsgeschichte* which shows forth God's relations with His creatures as a continuing theme down through the generations. That is, God brings the same truth and guidance always, but humans pervert it and refuse it and go astray ("but if they turn away, it is they who are in schism"). God warned and heard and observed in the past, and He does the same now. The Abrahamic emphasis in the Qurʾān was the crucial historico-theological foundation for the Muslim ummah, and as such it was an ideological triumph as well over the "cultured despisers"[18] of Muhammad's message and of his activity of forming a new religious community.

But even with the "over-againstness" which the ummah of Muhammad was to feel with regard to the People of the Book there was a willingness to recognize common convictions (see 3:64, "O People of the Book, come to a work (which is) fair between us and you (to wit) that we serve no one but Allah . . ."). It does not appear that the Muslims felt that they should

[18]The Jews of Yathrib. Friedrich Schleiermacher's famous epithet does not apply completely here if compared with its original context of late Englightenment Germany. But Muhammad did have a difficult task in dealing with a people with a long and learned religious and cultural tradition.

liquidate the Jews and Christians as such; in fact, in the Meccan and Medinan periods there was considerable toleration of them, and also for the Meccan heathen (see 45:14: "Tell those who believe to forgive those who hope not for the days of Allah; in order that He may requite folk what they used to earn"—Pickthall trans.). The Ummah is a forgiving and just community, and in this fact lies its capacity to mediate between people and to show forth in its very existence the forgiveness and justice of God. This is seen especially in the *ummah wasaṭ,* "midmost community," of 2:143. In 60:7–9 there is expressed the proper balance between forgiveness and resistance. This was delivered before the great expedition to Mecca:

> It is possible that Allah may appoint that there shall be love between you and those of them with whom ye have been at enmity; Allah is powerful, and Allah is forgiving, compassionate.
>
> Allah does not forbid you to act virtuously towards those who have not fought against you in the matter of religion, and have not expelled you from your dwellings, or to deal fairly with them—Allah loveth those who deal fairly.
>
> Allah simply forbids you to make friends of those who have fought against you in the matter of religion, and have expelled you from your dwellings, or have backed up your expulsion; whosoever makes friends of them—these are the wrong-doers.

There is no easy friendship between the Ummah and those outside, however. In fact, believers are not to have association with unbelievers, at least in a state of *jihād,* as seen above. As the years passed in Medina, the attitude toward the idolaters became increasingly severe in contrast to the earliest Meccan period, which really does not contain an attack upon paganism as such. But Muhammad and the Qur>ān took over many aspects of Arabian paganism and adapted them to the new religion. This was significant in that it provided a sense of continuity for the Ummah in relation to its Arabian ground, but subsumed all the features of the former times under the authority and sovereignty and especially the oneness of Allah.[19]

[19]See Watt, *Muhammad at Medina,* p. 313, where the author explains the preservation of belief in angels, jinn, demons, and so forth on the basis of their native "deep-rootedness" and "social utility." These two reasons are not to be denied, but the evolving cultus of Arabian Islam cannot be explained in these terms only, for to do so would be superficial and facile in a crudely functionalist manner. The arabization of Islam was not a purely calculated accomplishment. It was at least as much a fortuitous eventuality in which strong religious conviction concerning the divine will and activity was centrally operative. God conquered and subdued paganism through his prophet and through the emerging Muslim community, but he did not demolish the symbol system of pre-Islamic Arabia. Rather, he reoriented it and provided it with a new grounding. The making of a gracious land out of

### (b) An Ummah Muslimah

Abraham, according to 2:127–129, when he raised the foundation of the Kaᶜba along with his son Ishmael, prayed: "O our Lord, make us to be submissive to Thee, and of our posterity a community submissive to Thee [*wa min dhurrīyyātinā ummatan muslimatan laka*], and show us our rites, and relent towards us." A community submissive to the Lord was what Muhammad as prophet was gathering together. The mythic charter of the Ummah of Islam, the ummah muslimah, was seen to have been contained and expressed in Abraham's prayer. This term, ummah muslimah, designates Abraham's people in their formative context, as understood by the Qurʾānic record; but Abraham's people in this record are also Muhammad's people, and Muhammad's people are Abraham's people in the sense that they are the descendants who have risen upon God's guidance to fulfill the prayer of being a submissive community.

Submission to God entails a radical break with the customary psychological and ethical posture of the Arabs, who were a proud and passionate people, not given to humility and meekness. The taking on of the duty of absolute submission entailed a total turning over, or even a turning inside out of the self. This radical reversal of role and intention and customary behavior is expressed in terms like *tawbah,* "repentance," which is an important aspect of the act of *islām* and the preparation for *īmān* on the one hand, and the term which expresses in an affecting manner the quality of God's forgiveness, on the other. That is, God also "repents," not of course from weakness or error, but toward the benefit of His creatures. He relents, rather, or reverses His wrath (e.g., 9:15: "Allah relenteth [*yatūbu*] toward whom He will"—Pickthall trans.) because He wills mercy and forgiveness. This concept of repentance is important, then, both for the individual and the community, but also as divine activity. It is personal and volitional, and finally superior to justice, being an expression of mercy.[20]

Izutsu has argued that the Qurʾānic preaching brought about a revolution in the specification of what an authentic human life should consist in.[21] The pre-Islamic Arabs had been characterized by a basic dichotomy in personality

---

a contentious and fractious one was not achieved simply by recognizing "deep-rootedness" and "social utility." For example, the keeping of the Kaᶜba, without idols, was not a consolation prize for the defeated Meccans; it was an act of triumph, but a magnanimous triumph which meant not destruction but life and new beginnings. It also demonstrated God's authority over the past as well as the present and future, for the cleansing of the Kaᶜba by Muhammad was a rededication of it as the archetypal sanctuary reaching back to Abraham.

[20]See Frederick M. Denny, "The Qurʾānic Vocabulary of Repentance: Orientations and Attitudes," in Alford T. Welch, ed., *Studies in Qurʾān and Tafsīr* (Missoula, Montana: Scholars Press, 1980), pp. 649–664.

[21]*God and Man in the Koran,* chap. 8, "Jahiliyya and Islam."

and character between the concepts of *jahl* and *ḥilm,* between hot-blooded impetuosity and barbarousness, on one side, and calm self-control on the other.[22] These two traits were in a polar relationship in pre-Islamic times; after Muhammad, they were not totally eradicated, but rather transformed into the new polarity of *kufr-islām.* What the *jāhil* was in pre-Islamic times the *kāfir* was to be after Islam.[23] The jāhil was hostile and impetuous, blindly jealous of his honor (*ʿirḍ*); the kāfir is similarly wrapped up in himself and devoted to less than ultimate issues. The fact that this latter term also means "ingratitude" is significant: The one who is narrow and unbelieving and insensitive to the signs of God is, in sum, "ungrateful" to the Lord of his life and his reward. He is a churl. The *ḥalīm* person, however, is self-controlled and moderate as well as generous, a superior type whose virtue is a function of his power of character and personality.

Izutsu regards ḥilm as still operative and perhaps even dominant in the Qurʾān with regard to recommended relations between man and his fellows. But ḥilm cannot be recommended as man's proper attitude to God, anymore than jahl can. It is impossible to regard God from a jāhilī standpoint and be in a proper relationship with Him, for obvious reasons. But what about the alternative for the pre-Islamic Arab: ḥilm? It is not immediately apparent, perhaps, why ḥilm should also be rejected as a recommended attitude toward God. After all, this was the virtue of the superior man before Islam. Its use in poetry shows it to have been a noble and thoroughly admirable human trait.

Izutsu rightly considers the fundamental relationship between God and man to be the Lord-servant relation, God as "Lord" (*rabb*) and man as His "servant" (*ʿabd*).[24] The ḥalīm, however noble and admirable in his

[22]For a discussion of these and related terms and concepts, see Ignaz Goldziher's two classic articles in his *Muslim Studies,* Vol. I, trans. S. M. Stern (Chicago: Aldine Publishing Co., 1966): "*Muruwwa* and *Dīn,*" pp. 1–44, and "What is Meant by 'al-Jāhiliyya,'" pp. 201–208 (originally published in 1889.) Goldziher argued that jahl did not mean "ignorance" primarily, but "barbarism" and "arrogance." Edouard (Bishr) Farès, *L'Honneur chez les arabes avant l'Islam* (Paris: Adrien-Maisonneuve, 1932), contains a thorough discussion of the pre-Islamic concern for honor (*ʿirḍ*), and concludes that it was (and continued to be in tribal regions) the most important force for community life, not excluding Islam. The fullest and most satisfactory examination of jahl, ḥilm, and other terms is that of Izutsu, cited in the preceding note, upon which this discussion has drawn heavily.

[23]To a degree, at least. Actually, acting in a jāhil manner was not always to be despised in the old days, as long as it was not dominant in the life of an individual or group. Recall Goldziher's discussion: "*Jahl* thus was neither a virtue to the Arabs of an older time—it was appropriate to a young and impetuous character—nor was it entirely condemned. Part of the *muruwwa* ["manliness"] was knowing when mildness was not befitting the character of a hero and when *jahl* was indicated: 'I am ferocious (*jahūl*) where mildness (*taḥallum*) would make the hero despicable, meek (*ḥalīm*) when ferocity (*jahl*) would be unfitting to a noble.'" *Muslim Studies,* Vol. I, p. 205.

[24]*God and Man in the Koran,* p. 198.

self-control and balanced judgment, is no "servant," whether in relation to God or to his fellows:

> *Ḥalīm* is a man who knows how to smother his feelings, to overcome his own blind passions and to remain tranquil and undisturbed whatever happens to him, however much he may be provoked. . . .[25]

But ḥilm is not humble meekness, a passive virtue, the only recourse for the weak:

> On the contrary, it is a positive and active power of the soul that is strong enough to curb her own impetuosity that may drive the man headlong to folly, and calm it down to patience and forbearance. It is a sign of the power and superiority of the mind.[26]

Izutsu continues by illustrating that there must be power to produce ḥilm:

> It is essentially a quality of a man who governs and dominates others, and not of those who are governed and dominated. A naturally weak and powerless man is never called *ḥalīm,* however much he calms down his anger when insulted: he is "weak" simply.[27]

We can now perhaps understand why man does not regard God with ḥilm. Before Him man has no power, only weakness. However, that is no shame. God, on His side, is ḥalīm towards man (*al-Ḥalīm* is the thirty-third of the "most beautiful names of Allah").

The word ḥilm is actually missing from the Qurʾān, although the concept is clearly there. God (2:225, 235, 263; 3:155 and *passim*), Abraham (9:114; 11:75), Ishmael (37:101) and Shuʿayb (11:87) are all termed ḥalīm, but as Pellat has observed,[28] these instances mean "long-suffering," "patient," "gifted with tolerance," "slow to punish," all clearly Islamic virtues. Following Goldziher[29] in this matter, Pellat argues that ḥilm "must be the central feature of Islam,"[30] a judgment with which Izutsu agrees with respect to the Qurʾān's teaching concerning man's relation with his fellow men:

> In a certain sense the Koran as a whole is dominated by the very spirit of *ḥilm.* The constant exhortation to kindness (*iḥsān*) in human relations, the emphasis laid on justice (*ʿadl*), the forbidding of wrongful

[25] Ibid., p. 205.

[26] Ibid., p. 207.

[27] Ibid.

[28] Charles Pellat, "Ḥilm," *Encyclopedia of Islām,* New Edition, 4, 390–392. See also the same author's "Concept of *Hilm* in Islamic Ethics," *Bulletin of the Institute of Islamic Studies* (Aligarh Muslim University), nos. 6 and 7 (1962–1963), 1–12.

[29] *Muslim Studies,* Vol. I, p. 207 f.

[30] "Ḥilm," *EI,* 4, 390–392.

> violence (*ẓulm*), the bidding of abstinence and control of passions, the criticism of groundless pride and arrogance—all are concrete manifestations of this spirit of *ḥilm.*[31]

It is ḥilm, implicitly, of which the following passage speaks:

> The servants of the Merciful are those who walk humbly upon the earth, and, when the ignorant address them, say: "Peace." (25:63)

God is ḥalīm towards man, and the servants of the *Ḥalīm* are also, in turn, ḥalīm, but not toward God. Toward God, the servants are submissive, *muslims.* Ḥilm becomes the great ethical virtue of the ummah on the horizontal dimension, whereas on the vertical dimension, oriented toward God, there can only be islām and īmān, *shukr* and *taqwā,* and related expressions of man's subordinate and dependent position as creature and servant. In the days of the Jāhiliyya, men tended toward jahl or ḥilm in their interrelationships. But man was very much at the center of things, with no place for God. When Islam arose, this old polarity was challenged and replaced. Men were called to be servants (*ʿābidūn*), not of each other, but of a superior, overarching Power. The jāhil and the ʿabd are clearly contradictory types. But when jahl was banished as unsuitable in man's behavioral and attitudinal repertory, all that remained was its opposite, ḥilm.[32]

Ḥilm, as has been observed, is based on power, the superior mental and spiritual power of the individual human. But before the Lord, the ḥalīm man looks ludicrous. Ḥilm before God is, like jahl, the sin of *istikbār,* "arrogant pride" (e.g., see 71:7). Directed toward God, ḥilm is a form of *kufr,* not at all submissive or thankful. So ḥilm is an Islamic virtue only in inter*human* relations, and thus is at the core of ethics. With respect to God, it was superseded by Islam; or according to Izutsu, ḥilm was in a sense the "pre-religious, pre-Islamic form of *islām.*"[33] Not only can the man of special strength extend ḥilm to others for the promotion of serenity and stability; with Islam the ʿabd of God can also lay claim to ḥilm, because of the dignity and status which those who obey the Lord inherit—not the reserves of strength and courage which the unusual noble man possessed in Jāhiliyya times, but the courage and strength and substance of the Muslims which come in the covenant relationship with God. The Ummah is ḥalīm. It can afford to be, not because it possesses self-generated virtue (although it could be argued on functional grounds that it does),[34] but because it possesses

[31] *God and Man in the Koran,* p. 216.

[32] Ibid., p. 217.

[33] Ibid., p. 219.

[34] See, for example, Anthony F. C. Wallace, "Revitalization Movements," *American Anthropologist,* 58 (1956), 264–281.

charismatic power. "The servants of the Merciful are those who walk humbly upon the earth, and when the ignorant [*al-jāhilūn*] address them, say: 'Peace' " (25:63). True ḥilm, then, is possible only when the strength of God is possessed. No longer adequate was the rugged and often quite admirable force of character of individual noble Arabs, for as 96:3 asserts: "*Iqraʾ wa rabbuka-l-akram*" ("Recite: Thy Lord is the Most Noble").[35] In a world without God, as ancient Arabia may be characterized, human life was arranged and lived along lines of custom, with personal power and courage prime requisites for survival. It could be said that in those days the development of ḥilm and its universal admiration contributed to a sort of *praeparatio Evangelica,* a moral climate which could receive the news of God's ḥilm when it was understood, as it was, how great also was His power. The ummah muslimah, because of its servanthood to God, is thereby filled with ḥilm, for it is in covenant with ultimate power and generosity. Only the Muslim Ummah under Muhammad could have conquered Mecca and decide not to take terrible bloody vengeance on Quraysh. That was the act and the proof par excellence of ḥilm: the ḥilm of God and his people towards the ends of peace and salvation.

The ummah muslimah (and *wasaṭ*) is not submissive to the things of this world, however.

> O ye who have believed, what is the matter with you? When one says to you: "March out in the way of Allah," ye are weighed down to the ground; are ye so satisfied with this nearer life [*ad-dunyā*] as to neglect the Hereafter [*al-ākhirah*]? The enjoyment of this nearer life is in comparison with the Hereafter only a little thing. (9:38)

Marching out in the Way of Allah is hardly submissiveness with respect to the world. It is the expression of the will to subdue the world and bring it to the service of God. Before God the Ummah is submissive; but before the world it is active. The "Peace" which the "servants of the Merciful" announce to the ignorant and barbarous is not the capitulation of the weak, but the assurance of the strong. Those who join this ummah will enjoy *salām* in this world and the "reward most fair" in the next. The ummah muslimah, and wasaṭ then, is the community of falāḥ, the safe refuge of those who hold steadfastly to the "cable of Allah, and do not separate" (3:103) (Pickthall trans.), the covenant fellowship who believe they are destined for the eternal *dār as-salām*.

[35]I am indebted for this rendering to the late Professor Mohamed al-Nowaihi, who suggested that "most noble" is preferable to "most generous," because the former includes the latter while at the same time asserting a natural superiority. The proud Arabs with the bluest bloodlines still could not be in any way compared to God, who alone is essentially and uniquely *karīm*.

### (c) The "Best Community"

The Ummah as community of falāḥ is not an entity comprised of those who have only nominally submitted, whatever developed concepts after the Qur᾽ān might hold. Islam requires more than nominal affirmation; it requires right action and life. Being an ummah is not in itself sufficient for the salvation of a people. There have been many ummahs, according to the Qur᾽ān, some of which have perished after having been found lacking. But Muhammad's people are not an ummah muslimah only; they are the "best community ever produced for the people, urging what is reputable and restraining from what is disreputable, and believing in Allah" (3:110b). This "best community" is not the small sect of Meccan times, whose basic footing was in the pagan society of Qurayshi dominated life. It is the Ummah of Medina which was a complete social-political-religious system.

This essay has not seen as its task the investigation and analysis of the social and political structure of the Ummah of Medina as reflected in the Qur᾽ān or other sources. But it is necessary to point out that this ummah was not simply an ideal concept, as some of the terms which have been discussed might suggest; it was a *real* entity, also, and possessed the complexity and ambiguity of actual communities, religious or otherwise. Although the Qur᾽ān provides no systematic legal corpus, there is much in it pertaining to how humankind should rightly live in the Ummah: marital relations and family life, inheritance, commercial activities and relations, social welfare (e.g., *zakāt*), slaves, punishment for crimes, and so on, all of which and more are to be understood as implicit in the "urging what is reputable and restraining from what is disreputable," a key phrase for Qur᾽ānic ethics.

"You are the best *ummah*" (3:110) seems to have been revealed when Muhammad was having difficulties in Medina with the People of the Book, especially with the Jews. The context indicates this and the view is supported by classical scholars as well. The meaning, or at least part of the meaning, is that the Muslims are a more righteous people than those who have come before, particularly the Jews. The old ummahs fell into variance and were torn internally by dissension and strife (3:105). The "best *ummah*" is the ummah muslimah, which enjoins right conduct (*maʿrūf*) and forbids what is disreputable (*munkar*),[36] that is, it sees as of central importance a moral, legal, and juridical function, combined with sanctions derived from God's authority.

[36]On maʿrūf and munkar, see Izutsu, *Ethico-Religious Concepts,* pp. 213–217. Also, Hourani, "Ethical Presuppositions," pp. 14 f. The two terms seem to have meant, respectively, "what is recognized" and "what is rejected," either by pre-Islamic Arabian society, or by the Qur᾽ān, where, as Hourani suggests, "they appear to mean simply 'right' and 'wrong,' but they may have acquired fresh meanings of divine recognition and rejection."

The Muslim Ummah is considered the "best community" also perhaps because it is envisioned as a total community with a comprehensive world view comprising the social, political, economic, legal, cultural, and military aspects under a *religiously* grounded conception of order, security, and destiny, something which the previous ummahs never achieved. The ummah muslimah was not conceived as an *ekklesia,* a congregation "called out" of the large world (except perhaps in Mecca, before the Ummah proper was established by Muhammad). As the Constitution of Medina stated at the outset, "They [the believers] are a single *ummah* distinct from (other) people"; and the document clearly indicates that this community was to be a total social, political, and religious entity, a closed group not sharing open relationships of a significant nature (other than occasional bipartite treaties, though never alliances) with those outside, but always seeking to be unified, integral, and self-sufficient.

Maurice Causse has argued convincingly that Muhammad's message began in the early Meccan period as a "théologie de rupture" and evolved gradually by the Medinan period into a "théologie de la communauté."[37] The "théologie de rupture" was concerned with the orphan, the persecuted, the poor, in a denunciation of the present corrupt age upon which the light of God's greatness, mercy, and justice was being trained. The disvaluation of *ad-dunyā* as a transitory and perishable state is seen vividly in suras like 81, *At-Takwīr,* which apocalyptically judges the present order and foresees doom:

> When the sun shall be darkened,
> when the stars shall be thrown down,
> when the mountains shall be set moving,
> when the pregnant camels shall be neglected,
> when the savage beasts shall be mustered,
> when the seas shall be set boiling,
> when the souls shall be coupled,
> when the buried infant shall be asked for what sin
> she was slain,
> when the scrolls shall be unrolled,
> when the heaven shall be stripped off,
> when Hell shall be set blazing,
> when Paradise shall be brought nigh,
> *then* shall a soul know what it has produced.
>
> (81:1–14—Arberry trans., italics mine)

[37]"Théologie de rupture et théologie de la communauté," *Revue d'histoire et de philosophie religieuse,* 44 (1964), 60–80.

Max Weber has declined to call Islam a religion of salvation because it lacks a "tragic sense of sin."[38] He argues that Islam, in its early development and during the conquests, especially, was primarily a religion of political and economic concerns, with the Arab warrior class providing the ideal of leadership and manhood, after the charismatic model of Muhammad. The new military élite was armed with the conviction of superior virtue and the backing of a sovereign god who offers prosperity and success in this world and the assurance of a personal afterlife of a hedonistic sort, a "soldier's paradise." There is some value in Weber's all too brief treatment of Islam, but the failure to discern the peculiar quality that permeates the definitive Qur'ānic period of the Ummah's founding and early development is a serious error, caused mainly, it appears, by his preoccupation with religious disvaluations of the world, which he had analyzed in Buddhism, Christianity, and Hinduism. Weber's "tragic sense of sin," however real and important in religious history, is insufficient to serve as the sine qua non of all salvation doctrines. Weber designates the sin of the Arab context as basically connected with "feudal morality." It is true that ideas of right and wrong were closely linked with relationships among groups of people, for example, tribes. "Feudal morality" is a conspicuous feature of the Constitution of Medina, as it defines behavior in terms of loyalties and mutual defense; and the arrangement of arbitrations and sanctions is all finally linked to Muhammad as *rasūl Allah,* who himself was a sort of "vassal" of God. But the Qur'ānic record provides far greater richness and subtlety concerning the complexities of the human predicament and the ways in which man avoids acknowledging both his plight and his hope. "Feudal" man is still human and Causse's "théologie de rupture" is anything but an affirmation of the status quo. On the contrary, it is prophecy of a classical kind, speaking forth about man's condition and God's disposition.

No Arab would have ever thought of neglecting his she-camel in her time of parturition, not because of a sentimental attachment to the maddening but curiously beloved beast, but because the camel was one of the most important sources of wealth in that society. Fittingly, in the prophetic symbolism, the neglect of camels as envisioned in "The Darkening" (Sura 81) functions as an eschatological sign of reversal of the accepted "feudal morality," when there would be no time for an "interim ethic." The quoted passage takes on special poignancy, even tragedy, in the line about the girl infant who, at the Last Day, will be asked for what sin (*dhanb*) she was slain. The point is that she was slain for no "sin" at all, but

[38] *The Sociology of Religion,* trans. Ephraim Fischoff (Boston: Beacon Press, 1963), pp. 262 ff.

rather for a perverse reason somehow tied in with traditional tribal morality.[39] When all the signs have been revealed, including the one which indicates men's actions as having been tallied on concealed scrolls, "then a soul shall know what it has produced." This passage from *At-Takwīr* is far from an expression of feudal morality, and it would be easy to multiply examples of other passages like it. Muhammad's preaching, his theology of "rupture," again to use Causse's term, was designed to *penetrate* the old feudal morality of Mecca as well as the unjust social context in which even the good aspects of "tribal humanism," to use Watt's more sophisticated term, were deteriorating. The apodosis, "then a soul shall know what it has produced," is a dramatic statement of the individual's radical moral accountability, over which God's justice is supreme. The sin which Muhammad knew to be in the hearts of his fellow Arabs has been graphically illustrated in 68:51:

> The unbelievers well nigh strike thee down with their glances, when they hear the Reminder, and they say, 'Surely he is a man possessed!' And it is not but a reminder to all beings. (Arberry trans.)

Whether or not it was a tragic sense of sin, Muhammad certainly had a great concern for sin, ritual and moral. The Qur'ān contains a variety of terms and several types of sin of varying degrees of seriousness.[40] All sins, however, may ultimately be grouped under the general one of kufr, "unbelief," which, as we have seen, includes the notion of ingratitude to God.[41] Muhammad was convinced that the end of the world was at hand, at least the Qur'ān seems to express such a conviction at times (e.g., 21:2; 17:72); but by the Medinan period he was obviously more concerned with

[39]This is a vexed issue. See the extensive note in W. Robertson Smith, *Kinship and Marriage in Early Arabia,* with additional notes by the author and by Ignaz Goldziher, ed. Stanley A. Cook (Boston: Beacon Press, n.d.; based on the London edition of 1903), pp. 291–296, which contains among other things an attempt to explain the possible reasons behind Cais's murder of his grown daughter, which seems not to have been the usual one of penury, but possibly some fear of disgrace. See also Gertrude H. Stern, "Muhammad's Bond with the Women," *Bulletin of the School of Oriental and African Studies,* 10, Part I (1940–42), 193 f., where the author discredits Lammens's contention (in *Études sur le règne du Calife Omaiyade Mo'awia I^er^* [Beirut: Imprimerie Catholique, 1906–1908], p. 77, n. 3) that "Muhammad wished to acquire for himself the merit of abolishing the custom which was actually not wide-spread." The custom certainly was common enough, but by the time of Muhammad not general. The Qur'ān mentions the killing of children in 6:138, 16:58, 17:31, and 60:12, in addition to 80:8, where female infanticide is specified.

[40]For a brief summary of terminology, see Helmer Ringgren, "Sin and Forgiveness in the Koran," *Temenos,* 2 (1966), 98–111. A fuller study is W. R. W. Gardner, *The Qur'ānic Doctrine of Sin* (Madras: S.P.C.K. Press, Vepery, 1914). The most detailed recent discussion is that of Izutsu in *Ethico-Religious Concepts,* chaps. 7 and 8.

[41]Izutsu's position in *Ethico-Religious Concepts,* chaps. 7 and 8.

the establishment of a godly social order.[42] The period of "théologie de rupture" did call for conversion, but there was included in the teaching a strong sense of God's activity on behalf of humans as well.

Causse further argues, as have others, that the chief model for Muhammad among the prophets included in the Qur᾿ān was Moses. This is not to say that Abraham is less important in the total picture. Rather, Abraham is the model for the believers, whereas Moses is the model for prophecy, and especially for Muhammad's personal prophetic career.[43] The "hijra" (Exodus) of Moses (see Suras 20 and 26, especially) preceded, according to the Qur᾿ānic chronology, the actual *hijrah* of Muhammad and the Meccans among his followers. In Medina, the hijrah is explicitly connected with the Exodus, as may be seen in the Medinan suras which contain narratives of Moses (e.g., 2 and 7), so much so that we might call Muhammad "the Moses of the Arab people."[44] There is also an Abrahamic hijrah, a "going out" to a place where one is totally dependent upon God and where one has given up the supports of family, land, and tradition as being neither authentic nor lasting. Causse has considered all three hijrahs as responses to a spiritual requirement: "l'hégire est une loi de l'action prophétique et de l'oeuvre divine."[45] The requirement of hijrah is thus a communal *rite de passage*. One must be separated from this world in a kind of symbolic death, throwing oneself wholly on the resources of God, dwelling in tents as it were, before there can be a *réagrégation*.[46] Rupture is a liminal phase, absolutely essential before there can be a new life, in this case a life in a new community, a kind of rebirth into a society bent on success in covenant with God.

Watt has written that there is no real *rite de passage* into the Ummah on the individual level, either in the Qur᾿ān or in later Islam.[47] It could be argued, however, that the coming into being of the Ummah of Islam was itself a *rite de passage* for humankind, which Muhammad and the early heroes of the faith underwent to carry out God's will of bringing the "best community" into being, thus making possible authentic life through participation in a new social-religious and moral order.

[42] For a treatment of the Qur᾿ān message as a thoroughgoing eschatology, see Paul Casanova's interesting (but largely rejected) thesis, *Mohammed et la fin du monde* (Paris: Librairie Paul Geuthner, 1911–1924), which argues that Muhammad was influenced by a Christian sect with a doctrine of the nearness of the end of the world.

[43] Causse, p. 62.

[44] Ibid., p. 70.

[45] Ibid.

[46] See Arnold Van Gennep, *The Rites of Passage,* trans. M. B. Vizedom and B. L. Caffee (Chicago: University of Chicago Press, 1960; originally published in 1909).

[47] W. Montgomery Watt, "Conditions of Membership in the Islamic Community," *Studia Islamica,* 21 (1964), 12.

# INDEX